Also available from Houghton Mifflin in the Master Bridge Series

Test Your Card Play Volumes I & II by Hugh Kelsey

Killing Defense at Bridge by Hugh Kelsey

Instant Guide to Bridge by Hugh Kelsey and Ron Klinger

Bridge Basics by Ron Klinger

The Mistakes You Make at Bridge
by Terence Reese and Roger Trézel

Blocking, Unblocking and Safety Plays in Bridge
by Terence Reese and Roger Trézel

All You Need to Know about Play
by Terence Reese and David Bird

Playing to Win at Bridge by Ron Klinger

100 Winning Bridge Tips by Ron Klinger

Improve Your Bridge Memory by Ron Klinger

Five-Card Majors by Ron Klinger

Simple Squeezes

It is widely acknowledged that the ability to recognize and execute squeezes at the bridge table is the hallmark of the expert. Yet squeeze play, far from being difficult, is well within the grasp of any competent player, as grand master Hugh Kelsey explains with his customary lucidity. Distilling the experience of a lifetime and the essence of thousands of bridge hands within the covers of this book, the author clearly sets out the requirements for all the basic simple squeezes, those most commonly met with at the table.

All the example hands are instructive and many are brilliant. Accomplished players who think they know it all may be surprised to discover how much they still have to learn. Those keen on improving will find a new dimension opening up before them. The book will serve as their passport to a magical and exciting world of squeeze play, helping to lift their game to an altogether higher level.

The author points out in his introduction that a knowledge of squeeze play can turn you into a more complete card player, a more desirable partner, and more formidable opponent. Need we say more?

"Exciting book . . . should be useful and instructive for those players who still believe that a squeeze is a mysterious part of bridge."

— Rixi Marcus, *Guardian*

SIMPLE
SQUEEZES

Hugh Kelsey

*A Master Bridge Series title
in conjunction with Peter Crawley*

Houghton Mifflin Company
Boston   New York   1995

For information about permission to reproduce selections from this book,
write to Permissions, Houghton Mifflin Company, 215 Park Avenue South,
New York, New York 10003.

Library of Congress Cataloging-in-Publication Data

Simple squeezes / Hugh Kelsey.
p. cm. — (A Master Bridge Series Title)
Originally published: London : V. Gollancz in association
with P. Crawley, 1985. With new introd.
ISBN 0-395-72858-4
1. Contract bridge — Squeeze. 2. Contract bridge — Collections
of games. I. Title. II. Series: Master bridge series.
GV1282.44.K45 1995   94-45166
795.41'53 — dc20   CIP

Printed in the United States of America
BP 10 9 8 7 6 5 4 3 2 1

Contents

Introduction	*page*	7
How the Machinery Works		9
The Positional Squeeze		12
The Automatic Squeeze		26
Overcoming a Blockage		46
The Ruffing Squeeze		56
Squeeze Defence		70
Exercises		90

Introduction

Many players are content to spend a lifetime at the card table without discovering what squeeze play is all about. When the subject of squeezing comes up in conversation they feel a little uncomfortable, of course. All they can do is nod unhappily and try to look wise. Such players may play a perfectly respectable game, enjoying their bridge and having their share of wins. But they don't win as often as they would like to, and they suspect that they are missing out on a secret source of pleasure. In fact they are denying themselves the most exhilarating moments that the game has to offer.

Everyone knows what a squeeze feels like from the receiving end. To the uninitiated the whole business smacks of black magic. How is it possible for declarer to make our sure winners disappear into thin air like that? And how dare he, anyway? It can be hard to believe that squeeze play is just a normal extension of card-play technique—a skill that can be acquired with practice.

The only way to beat the squeezers is to join them. The education of a bridge player is incomplete until he has acquired a working knowledge of squeeze play, and for improving players there is no more rewarding area of study in the whole field of card play. What puts some people off is that it is necessary to work at the subject. There are many positions, each with its own requirements as to the placing of entries and menaces, and it is only by doing your homework in advance that you can hope to recognise a squeeze position when you come across it in practical play.

There is certainly a lot to learn and you may despair of ever getting the hang of the subject. But the rewards of perseverance are sure. One day you will find yourself making an 'impossible' contract by means of a squeeze which you have planned from the start. Then you will know the supreme thrill of our game.

From that moment there will be no turning back, for you will have discovered that squeezes are not just hard work but great fun. You will start looking for squeezes on every hand and you will find them often enough to keep your enthusiasm alive. You will have become a more complete card player, a more desirable partner and a more dangerous opponent.

This book can be your introduction to the magical world of squeeze play. It deals with those squeezes that are most often encountered in play—simple squeezes against one opponent in two suits. In later books in this series we shall explore some of the more complex squeezes. Meanwhile—read, absorb and enjoy!

1

How the Machinery Works

An understanding of squeeze play can be acquired only by starting from first principles and examining the basic machinery. I trust those who already have some knowledge of the elements of the squeeze will bear with me for a few pages. We had better start by defining our terms. There have been many attempts to define a squeeze, but in my view the only sensible definition is the one that covers all possibilities—a squeeze occurs when a player is compelled to make a discard that is disadvantageous to his side. This may appear at the moment to be a loose and haphazard definition, but as we progress I hope you will come to see that it is the only acceptable one.

The simple squeeze—the subject of this book—is the squeeze of one opponent in two suits. Let us consider how such a squeeze might arise.

All squeeze play is made possible by the fact that declarer and dummy between them hold twice as many cards as either one of the defenders. If the cards of one defender are useless, his partner, charged with the task of keeping winners or stoppers in two suits, may find the job too much for him. Outflanked by the sheer mass of the menaces surrounding him, he may be compelled to release a card that is damaging to the defence. Consider the following diagram.

Simple Squeezes

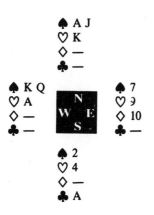

♠ A J
♡ K
◇ —
♣ —

♠ K Q
♡ A
◇ —
♣ —

♠ 7
♡ 9
◇ 10
♣ —

♠ 2
♡ 4
◇ —
♣ A

Here West has the task of protecting both hearts and spades, and when the ace of clubs is led he cannot cope. Either a spade or the ace of hearts has to be discarded, and both choices are disastrous.

Dummy, discarding after West, can throw the card that is no longer needed. If West parts with a spade, dummy discards the king of hearts. If West throws the heart ace, dummy naturally discards the spade jack. Either way, declarer makes the rest of the tricks.

All the essential features of the simple squeeze are apparent in the above diagram. Let us examine them one at a time, giving each due consideration. These basic features are interdependent and if any one is absent the squeeze will fail.

Squeeze Card. This is the card that applies pressure to the defender—the ace of clubs in the above diagram. Normally the squeeze card is a winner in a free suit—that is a suit not involved in the squeeze. Often the squeeze card is declarer's last trump, or the last of a string of winners at no trumps.

Menaces. These are cards held by declarer or dummy which may be promoted to winning rank by the forced discard of the defender. There are a number of points to note about menaces.

1. The same defender must be threatened in two suits, and one of the menaces must be accompanied by a card of winning rank. In the above diagram West's ace of hearts is menaced by the king in dummy, and the king and queen of spades are threatened by the ace and jack. The heart king is termed a one-card menace against West, while the ace and jack of spades constitute a two-card menace. Note that a two-card m㎎ce consists of a master card and a loser in the same suit.

2. At least one of the menaces must lie 'over' the defender to be squeezed. In other words, if West is to be squeezed one of the menaces must be in the North hand, while if East is to be squeezed one of the menaces must lie in the South hand.

3. The two-card menace must lie in the hand opposite the squeeze card. The reason for this becomes apparent when we look at the next requirement for the squeeze.

Entries. There is no point in forcing a defender to discard a winner unless you have some means of access to the established menace in the hand opposite the squeeze card. The master card of the two-card menace provides the required entry. It follows that in order to complete the link you must have a small card of the same suit in the hand that contains the squeeze card. In the diagram on the opposite page we could exchange the four of hearts for a small diamond without damaging the position, but the two of spades is vital. Take it away and the squeeze will fail.

Timing. If you examine West's cards in the diagram you will see that they are all performing a vital role at the time when the squeeze card is led. They are all 'busy' cards, in other words. This must always be the case if the squeeze is to succeed, since by definition the forced discard must damage the defender's hand.

Turn your attention to the North and South cards in the diagram and you will see that of the three remaining tricks the declarer has two winners and just the one loser. This is an essential feature of the basic squeeze. At the point when the squeeze card is led, declarer must be in a position to win all the remaining tricks except one. He must have no more than one loser when the squeeze card is led. For this reason the basic squeezes are sometimes referred to as one-loser squeezes.

Suppose we alter the last diagram by adding a small diamond to each hand.

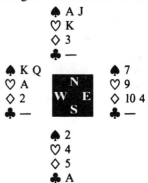

♠ A J
♡ K
◊ 3
♣ —

♠ K Q
♡ A
◊ 2
♣ —

♠ 7
♡ 9
◊ 10 4
♣ —

♠ 2
♡ 4
◊ 5
♣ A

In this four-card ending South still has two winners but he also has two losers and it is clear that the squeeze does not work. The extra loser creates space for an idle card in the defender's hand.

West happily discards the two of diamonds on the ace of clubs and thus escapes the pressure of the squeeze.

It follows that when you are planning a squeeze you must time the play carefully, conceding the required number of tricks in the early stages in order to bring your loser count down to one. This process is known as 'rectifying the count.'

We have discovered four essential points in the operation of a simple squeeze—squeeze card, menaces, entries and timing. These four features, and the conditions that apply to each, must be engraved on the memories of all those who aspire to success at squeeze play.

2

The Positional Squeeze

Many plays at bridge succeed by virtue of the position of the enemy cards. The finesse is a simple example. When a low card is led towards an A Q in dummy, declarer can make two tricks if the king is in the right place, since West has to commit himself before a card is played from dummy. If East has the king the finesse fails.

A large group of simple squeezes makes use of the same positional factor. We saw in the last chapter that the two-card menace must always lie in the hand opposite the squeeze card. When the one-card menace is also opposite the squeeze card, we have what is known as a positional squeeze. Let us take another look at the diagram.

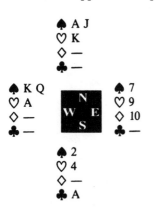

Clearly this squeeze depends on the position of the enemy stoppers, which are trapped between the squeeze card and the menaces in dummy. On the play of the ace of clubs West is forced to unguard one of the major suits. Dummy, playing after West, can hang on to the menace card that has been promoted and discard the other one.

Like the finesse, the positional squeeze depends for its success on finding the enemy cards well placed. Interchange the East and West cards, as in the next diagram, and the squeeze does not work.

Here dummy has to play ahead of East and dummy feels the pressure first. When the ace of clubs is played, one of the menace cards in dummy has to be discarded, and East avoids the pinch by following dummy's discard.

If you remember our second rule about menaces from the last chapter, you will realise that this squeeze is bound to fail since neither of the menaces lies 'over' East.

```
        ♠ A J
        ♡ K
        ◇ —
        ♣ —
♠ 7    N    ♠ K Q
♡ 9  W   E  ♡ A
◇ 10   S    ◇ —
♣ —         ♣ —
        ♠ 2
        ♡ 4
        ◇ —
        ♣ A
```

The value of the positional squeeze is limited by the fact that it is effective only against the player to the left of the squeeze card. Nevertheless, it is one of the most common forms of squeeze. Hands like the following are encountered every day.

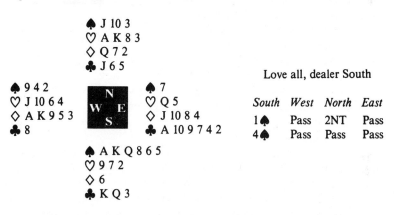

```
            ♠ J 10 3
            ♡ A K 8 3
            ◇ Q 7 2
            ♣ J 6 5
♠ 9 4 2    N    ♠ 7
♡ J 10 6 4  W   E  ♡ Q 5
◇ A K 9 5 3  S   ◇ J 10 8 4
♣ 8             ♣ A 10 9 7 4 2
            ♠ A K Q 8 6 5
            ♡ 9 7 2
            ◇ 6
            ♣ K Q 3
```

Love all, dealer South

South	West	North	East
1♠	Pass	2NT	Pass
4♠	Pass	Pass	Pass

West leads the king of diamonds and switches to the eight of clubs. East takes the ace and returns a club for his partner to ruff, and West gets off lead with a heart to the ace. How should you proceed?

The first step, not just for squeeze purposes but in the planning of any bridge hand, is to count your winners. Six trumps, two hearts and a club give you a total of nine tricks. You note ruefully that you would have had ten tricks but for that unkind enemy ruff in clubs. Now the only chance for a tenth trick lies with a squeeze. The timing is right, for the defenders have already taken three tricks and you can win all the remaining tricks except one.

[13]

Can you identify the menaces? The queen of diamonds will serve as a one-card menace against West, who is marked with the ace, and the two-card menace will have to be the king and eight of hearts. The contract can be made only if West began with long hearts as well as the top diamonds. Naturally you cannot be sure that West has four hearts, but there is nothing else to play for. The entry position is satisfactory with the two-card menace opposite the squeeze card, which will be the king of clubs. Just run all the trumps and reduce to this three-card ending:

Really you might succeed without knowing anything about squeeze play, for it is natural to run the trumps and reduce to this position. When the king of clubs is played West is unable to withstand the pressure of the squeeze. If he discards a heart, you throw the queen of diamonds from dummy and make the last two tricks in hearts. If West throws the ace of diamonds, you discard the small heart from the table and dummy is high.

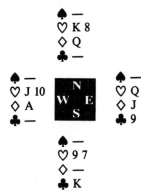

```
              ♠ —
              ♡ K 8
              ♢ Q
              ♣ —
♠ —                        ♠ —
♡ J 10    ┌───────┐        ♡ Q
♢ A       │   N   │        ♢ J
♣ —       │ W   E │        ♣ 9
          │   S   │
          └───────┘
              ♠ —
              ♡ 9 7
              ♢ —
              ♣ K
```

Players are sometimes discouraged from a study of squeeze play by the idea that prodigious efforts of memory are required. Nothing could be further from the truth. In the simple squeeze the demands on your concentration are very small.

In this hand, for instance, there is no need to pay attention to the discards in the heart suit, no need to count hearts at all. The only card you need to watch out for is the ace of diamonds. After West has played to the squeeze card, if the ace of diamonds has not appeared you simply discard the queen of diamonds and hope for the best in hearts.

This is the correct action in all basic squeeze play. Watch only for the card (or cards) that can beat your one-card menace and leave the long menace to look after itself. Remember that in a positional squeeze the one-card menace is always discarded on the squeeze card unless it has been promoted to winning rank.

EXTENDED MENACES

The usual form of long menace is a two-card menace, but it can be extended to three or even four cards without affecting the working of the

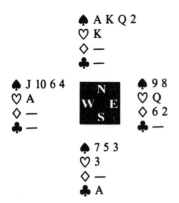

squeeze. Here is an example.

Instead of a two-card menace in the hand opposite the squeeze card there is a four-card menace, but the squeeze functions as before. Note that a four-card menace consists of three winners and one loser. In this ending declarer has four winners out of the last five tricks, so the timing of the squeeze is correct. The position could have been reduced to the more familiar matrix if declarer had been able to cash two top spades at an earlier stage. Sometimes this is not possible for one reason or another.

Are there any other permissible variations in the length of the menaces? Yes, the one-card menace can also be increased in length by the addition of cards of master rank without affecting the nature of the squeeze.

This time there are two three-card menaces opposite the squeeze card. Since West is the only defender guarding the major suits he is squeezed as before on the play of the ace of clubs.

In theory this arrangement of menaces is as effective as any other, but in practice it is highly undesirable. The reason is that when West discards on the ace of clubs it may not be at all easy to tell which suit he has unguarded. West need not, for

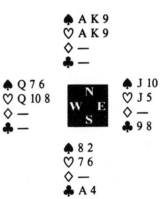

instance, have retained three cards in each major suit in the above diagram. Seeing what was coming, he might have discarded down to Q x in one of the majors at an earlier stage in order to mislead you. The ambiguity inherent in the situation may cause you to discard the wrong menace card from dummy, thus ruining your squeeze.

If you had cashed the top cards in one of the majors at an earlier stage in the play, this danger would not exist. You would know that there was only one heart (or spade) outstanding, and if West did not cough it up on the play of the ace of clubs you would know what to do.

To summarise, you always need to have one two-card or longer menace opposite the squeeze card, but it is a positive disadvantage to have a second one. Try to reduce one of the menaces to one card, thus avoiding ambiguity in the ending.

Here is the hand which might, but should not, give rise to the above diagram.

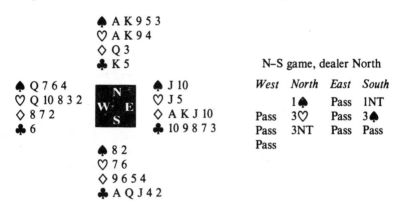

♠ A K 9 5 3
♡ A K 9 4
◇ Q 3
♣ K 5

N-S game, dealer North

♠ Q 7 6 4
♡ Q 10 8 3 2
◇ 8 7 2
♣ 6

♠ J 10
♡ J 5
◇ A K J 10
♣ 10 9 8 7 3

♠ 8 2
♡ 7 6
◇ 9 6 5 4
♣ A Q J 4 2

West	North	East	South
	1♠	Pass	1NT
Pass	3♡	Pass	3♠
Pass	3NT	Pass	Pass
Pass			

West finds the diamond lead and East takes his tricks, West discarding a heart and dummy two spades. East then plays the ten of clubs to dummy's king. How should you continue?

Naturally you hope that the clubs will be worth five tricks. If they are not, the only remaining chance is a major-suit squeeze against West, and to avoid guesswork in the ending you should play off the top cards in one of the majors before coming to hand with a second club.

Cash the ace and king of spades (say), and then run the clubs to reach this ending.

Now you have no problem in reading West's discards. If the queen of spades does not appear when the ace of clubs is played, you discard the spade nine from dummy and run the hearts.

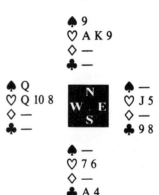

♠ 9
♡ A K 9
◇ —
♣ —

♠ Q
♡ Q 10 8
◇ —
♣ —

♠ —
♡ J 5
◇ —
♣ 9 8

♠ —
♡ 7 6
◇ —
♣ A 4

THE SPLIT TWO-CARD MENACE

There is one other type of menace that can be useful in positional squeeze play. The normal two-card menace consists of winner and small card opposite a singleton. But the elements of the two-card menace may be divided between the two hands, provided that the winner is still in the hand opposite the squeeze card.

If South had held a singleton spade, the two-card menace in dummy would not be effective. West could safely throw a spade on the ace of clubs, relying on his partner to control the second round of the suit. The fact that South has two spades, the top one of higher rank than either of East's cards, saves the day. West is squeezed as before on the play of the club ace.

The type of menace seen in the spade position above is called a split two-card menace. It is by no means uncommon and can be very useful in positional squeeze play. Here is an example.

♠ A 7
♡ K
◇ —
♣ —

♠ K 10   ♠ J 3
♡ A   ♡ 6
◇ —   W E   ◇ —
♣ —   ♣ —

♠ Q 5
♡ —
◇ —
♣ A

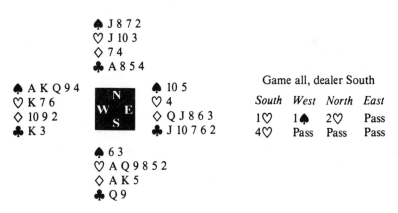

♠ J 8 7 2
♡ J 10 3
◇ 7 4
♣ A 8 5 4

♠ A K Q 9 4   ♠ 10 5
♡ K 7 6   ♡ 4
◇ 10 9 2   ◇ Q J 8 6 3
♣ K 3   ♣ J 10 7 6 2

♠ 6 3
♡ A Q 9 8 5 2
◇ A K 5
♣ Q 9

Game all, dealer South

South	West	North	East
1♡	1♠	2♡	Pass
4♡	Pass	Pass	Pass

West cashes the king and queen of spades and switches to the ten of diamonds. You ruff the third round of diamonds with dummy's jack of hearts and run the heart ten. West wins with the king and exits with a trump.

[17]

Needing the rest of the tricks, you have to hope that West can be squeezed in the black suits. Prospects are good, for the fact that West did not lead a club affords a strong presumption that he has the king.

Dummy's jack of spades will serve as the one-card menace, and the long menace will be the split two-card menace in clubs. The master card of the split two-card menace is in the hand opposite the squeeze card (the last trump), so there should be no problems. Just run the trumps, watching for the ace of spades. West must succumb when the last heart is played in this ending:

Mind you, West really brought all this trouble down upon his own head. We shall look again at this hand when we come to consider defending against squeezes.

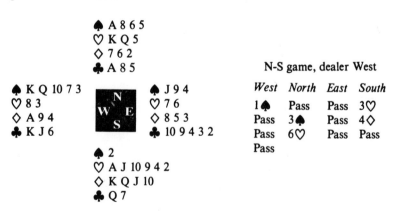

```
                ♠ J
                ♡ —
                ◇ —
                ♣ A 8
    ♠ A                    ♠ —
    ♡ —        N           ♡ —
    ◇ —     W     E        ◇ —
    ♣ K 3      S           ♣ J 10 7
                ♠ —
                ♡ 5
                ◇ —
                ♣ Q 9
```

ISOLATING THE MENACE

The menaces required for a squeeze are not always immediately to hand. Often a little preparatory work is needed to establish a menace against a particular defender.

```
              ♠ A 8 6 5
              ♡ K Q 5
              ◇ 7 6 2
              ♣ A 8 5
 ♠ K Q 10 7 3            ♠ J 9 4
 ♡ 8 3         N         ♡ 7 6
 ◇ A 9 4    W     E      ◇ 8 5 3
 ♣ K J 6       S         ♣ 10 9 4 3 2
              ♠ 2
              ♡ A J 10 9 4 2
              ◇ K Q J 10
              ♣ Q 7
```

N-S game, dealer West

West	North	East	South
1♠	Pass	Pass	3♡
Pass	3♠	Pass	4◇
Pass	6♡	Pass	Pass
Pass			

West leads the king of spades to dummy's ace. How should you plan the play?

[18]

You can count only eleven tricks and must hope to squeeze West in the black suits, using the split two-card menace in clubs as the long menace. At the moment you do not have an effective one-card menace in spades, for it is likely that East will have at least one card above the eight in rank. But if West began with five spades it should be possible to ruff out East's stopper, establishing dummy's eight as a real threat against West. This process is known as isolating the menace.

Draw trumps with the jack and queen, ruff a spade and then play a diamond. You have to knock out the ace of diamonds before ruffing another spade, otherwise West will be in a position to wipe out your menace with a fourth round of spades when he comes in with the diamond ace. Once the ace of diamonds has gone you can arrange to ruff a third spade, thus ensuring that only West can guard the black suits (you know he has the club king, of course, from his opening bid). Now the play of the red cards will apply irresistible pressure.

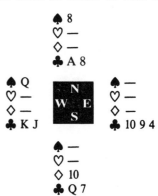

West is stuck for a discard when the ten of diamonds is played. Whether he parts with the queen of spades or a club, you make the rest of the tricks and your slam.

RECTIFYING THE COUNT

In the hands we have looked at so far the timing has been just right for a squeeze; the declarer has been in a position to take all the remaining tricks but one. Naturally this will not always be the case. When there are two or more losers, declarer has to resort to the technique known as 'rectifying the count', or 'adjusting the duke', as a Scottish colleague once whimsically put it.

'Rectifying the count' means conceding one or more tricks to the defenders until the timing is right for a squeeze—until the loser count comes down to one, in fact. Usually the rectification is done by holding up when the defenders attempt to establish their suit. Here is an example.

```
          ♠ 9 7 6 2
          ♡ K 5 2
          ◇ A K 7 4
          ♣ K J
```

Game all, dealer South

```
♠ K 10 8 4 3        ♠ Q J
♡ 8 7 4       N     ♡ 10 9 6 3
◇ J 10 6 2  W   E   ◇ Q 8
♣ 8           S     ♣ 9 7 5 3 2

          ♠ A 5
          ♡ A Q J
          ◇ 9 5 3
          ♣ A Q 10 6 4
```

South	West	North	East
1♣	Pass	1◇	Pass
2NT	Pass	4NT	Pass
6NT	Pass	Pass	Pass

West leads the four of spades and East plays the jack. How do you plan the play?

You have just eleven top tricks and the opponents have hit your weak spot. It looks as though the twelfth trick will have to come from a squeeze, which will be possible if West has five or more spades along with four or more diamonds. It may not be very likely, but you have nothing else to play for. Dummy's nine of spades will be the one-card menace and the diamonds will serve as the long menace.

What about the timing? At the moment you have two losers, and you know the squeeze will not work if you have more than one. Clearly you must rectify the loser count by conceding a trick to the defence, and the only opportunity you will have of conceding a trick is right now—at trick one.

Allow East to win the first trick with the jack of spades. You can win the spade continuation, unblock the king and jack of clubs, take three rounds of hearts, finishing in hand, and run the rest of the clubs, watching only for the spades that can beat dummy's nine.

West is squeezed on the play of the last club. If you had wished, you could have played off one round of diamonds when you were in dummy without affecting the operation of

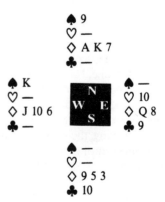

```
          ♠ 9
          ♡ —
          ◇ A K 7
          ♣ —
♠ K              ♠ —
♡ —      N       ♡ 10
◇ J 10 6 W   E   ◇ Q 8
♣ —        S     ♣ 9
          ♠ —
          ♡ —
          ◇ 9 5 3
          ♣ 10
```

the squeeze, but this was by no means essential. The important thing was that there should not be winners in both menace suits at the time the squeeze card was played.

Be sure to see that the squeeze would have failed if you had won the first trick. The end position would then have been as follows:

On the last club West can ditch his king of spades (he knows his partner has the queen, since the jack forced out your ace on the first round).

Now there is no way for you to avoid the loss of two tricks in the endgame.

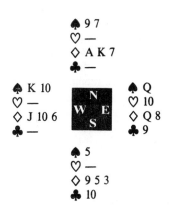

```
            ♠ 9 7
            ♡ —
            ◇ A K 7
            ♣ —
♠ K 10              ♠ Q
♡ —        N       ♡ 10
◇ J 10 6  W   E    ◇ Q 8
♣ —        S       ♣ 9
            ♠ 5
            ♡ —
            ◇ 9 5 3
            ♣ 10
```

It is usually a matter of holding up an ace when you need to rectify the count, but having held it up you may still need to cash the ace at a fairly early stage in order to avoid ambiguity. Here is an example.

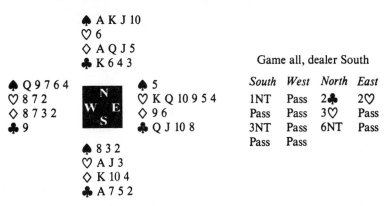

```
              ♠ A K J 10
              ♡ 6
              ◇ A Q J 5
              ♣ K 6 4 3             Game all, dealer South

♠ Q 9 7 6 4        ♠ 5
♡ 8 7 2     N      ♡ K Q 10 9 5 4
◇ 8 7 3 2  W   E   ◇ 9 6
♣ 9         S      ♣ Q J 10 8
              ♠ 8 3 2
              ♡ A J 3
              ◇ K 10 4
              ♣ A 7 5 2
```

South	West	North	East
1NT	Pass	2♣	2♡
Pass	Pass	3♡	Pass
3NT	Pass	6NT	Pass
Pass	Pass		

It's not the greatest of contracts, but this is the sort of thing that happens when your partner is playing a variable no trump and you are playing weak all the time.

West leads the eight of hearts and East puts in the queen. You can count only nine top tricks and you need the spade finesse to give you any chance at all. The twelfth trick can come only from a squeeze against East in hearts and clubs. You must hope that East has at least three clubs along with his long hearts.

A trick has to be conceded to rectify the count, so you permit East to hold the first trick. East switches to the queen of clubs, posing a secondary problem—whether to win this trick in hand or in dummy. It is not too hard to reach the right conclusion. Since dummy has the length in both spades and diamonds, the squeeze card must be on the table. The long squeeze menace must therefore be in your own hand. You must preserve the ace of clubs and win the second trick with dummy's king. After a diamond to your ten you try a spade finesse which passes off successfully. You return to hand with the diamond king and now, in order to avoid ambiguity, you must cash the ace of hearts before taking a second spade finesse. The run of the spades followed by the diamonds will cause East pain in the diagram position:

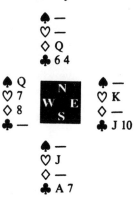

I hope the reason for cashing the ace of hearts earlier is clear to everyone. At double dummy it is not necessary, for the squeeze functions whether the ace of hearts has been cashed or not. But when you are playing a hand you do not normally have double-dummy knowledge of the location of the enemy cards and it is desirable to avoid guesswork whenever possible.

Suppose you had kept the ace of hearts in your hand and just run the spades and the diamonds. This is the sort of thing that is apt to happen to you.

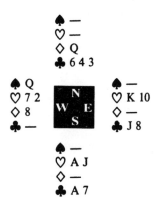

East has craftily thrown his ten of clubs at an earlier stage. When you play the last diamond from dummy he follows up his deception by discarding the ten of hearts, and you have a nasty guess to make. If you take the view that East has given up his club guard, you will discard the jack of hearts on the last diamond and go one down.

THE 'COUNT' SQUEEZE

Sometimes a knowledge of elementary squeeze play can protect you from a losing finesse.

Consider the following hand:

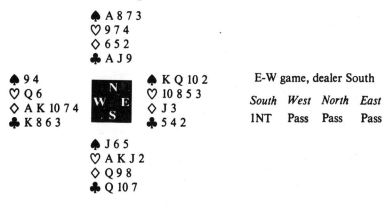

```
              ♠ A 8 7 3
              ♡ 9 7 4
              ◇ 6 5 2
              ♣ A J 9
♠ 9 4                          ♠ K Q 10 2
♡ Q 6                          ♡ 10 8 5 3
◇ A K 10 7 4                   ◇ J 3
♣ K 8 6 3                      ♣ 5 4 2
              ♠ J 6 5
              ♡ A K J 2
              ◇ Q 9 8
              ♣ Q 10 7
```

E-W game, dealer South

South	West	North	East
1NT	Pass	Pass	Pass

West leads the king of diamonds on which East plays the jack. West switches to the nine of spades, and when you play low from dummy the queen wins. Back comes a diamond giving West four more tricks in the suit. You discard two spades from dummy and a heart and a club from hand, while East throws a card from each suit. Next comes a spade to dummy's ace. You play a heart to your ace and return the queen of clubs which is covered by the king and ace. What now?

No player with the slightest knowledge of squeeze play will consider taking the heart finesse. If the finesse is working there is no need to take it. East is known to have the king of spades, and if he also has the queen of hearts it can be squeezed out of him. Just finish the clubs.

On the play of the last club East throws the heart eight, so you discard the one-card menace, the jack of spades. When you play a heart from dummy and East follows with the ten, you know that his remaining card is the king of spades. So you go up with the king of hearts and receive your bonus when the queen drops.

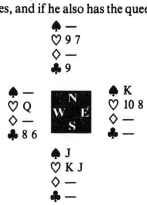

```
              ♠ —
              ♡ 9 7
              ◇ —
              ♣ 9
♠ —                    ♠ K
♡ Q                    ♡ 10 8
◇ —                    ◇ —
♣ 8 6                  ♣ —
              ♠ J
              ♡ K J
              ◇ —
              ♣ —
```

THE TRANSFER SQUEEZE

When it seems unlikely that the right defender will have stoppers in both key suits, there is no need to despair. It may be possible to transfer control from one defender to the other.

Here is an example:

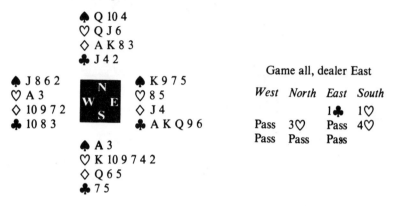

```
                ♠ Q 10 4
                ♡ Q J 6
                ◇ A K 8 3
                ♣ J 4 2
                                    Game all, dealer East
  ♠ J 8 6 2         ♠ K 9 7 5
  ♡ A 3       N     ♡ 8 5         West  North  East  South
  ◇ 10 9 7 2 W   E  ◇ J 4                        1♣   1♡
  ♣ 10 8 3      S   ♣ A K Q 9 6   Pass   3♡    Pass   4♡
                ♠ A 3            Pass   Pass   Pass
                ♡ K 10 9 7 4 2
                ◇ Q 6 5
                ♣ 7 5
```

The defence starts with three rounds of clubs. You ruff high on the third round and play a trump, West taking the ace and returning the three. What now?

You have ten top tricks if the diamonds break. If not you will have to rely on a squeeze. The spade and diamond menaces are both in dummy, and the only squeeze available is a positional one against West. That will work well if West has four diamonds and the king of spades, but on the bidding the king of spades is much more likely to be in the East hand. West could have the jack of spades, however, in which case it might be possible to transfer control of the spade suit to him.

Win the second trump in dummy and play the queen of spades. East must cover with the king and your ace wins the trick. Now the ten of spades is established as an effective one-card menace if West happens to hold the jack of spades, and you can try for the squeeze by running your trumps.

As it happens West has the jack of spades and the diamond stopper. On the play of the last heart he has to abandon his guard in one of the suits and you make the rest of the tricks.

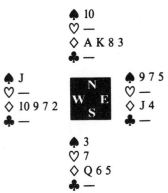

♠ 10
♥ —
♦ A K 8 3
♣ —

♠ J   ♠ 9 7 5
♥ —   ♥ —
♦ 10 9 7 2   ♦ J 4
♣ —   ♣ —

♠ 3
♥ 7
♦ Q 6 5
♣ —

3

The Automatic Squeeze

In squeeze play the menaces may both lie in the hand opposite the squeeze card, as in the positional squeeze, or one menace may lie in each hand. In the latter case we have what is known as the automatic squeeze. In the form most commonly encountered the one-card menace is in the same hand as the squeeze card and the long menace is in the opposite hand.

When the ace of clubs is played the two of hearts is thrown from dummy and East is squeezed. In an automatic squeeze one of the menaces lies over each defender, hence pressure can be applied to either defender. If the East and West cards are interchanged in the diagram, West will be squeezed instead of East.

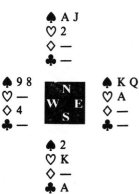

The difference between positional and automatic squeezes can be summarised as follows. In the positional squeeze, where both menaces lie opposite the squeeze card, one of the menaces has to be discarded on the squeeze card. The choice is dependent on the discard of the defender.

In automatic squeeze play the hand opposite the squeeze card is relieved of the burden of holding both menaces. Consequently there is always an idle card that can be thrown on the squeeze card irrespective of the card played by the defender. This is what enables the squeeze to operate against either defender.

Clearly the automatic squeeze is the less restricted form and one would expect its frequency to be roughly twice that of the positional squeeze. This is borne out in practice, and if there is a choice between a positional and an automatic squeeze you should opt for the more flexible automatic form by arranging for the menaces to be divided between the two hands.

Suppose we interchange the king and the two of hearts in the last diagram.

At first glance it has the appearance of a positional squeeze, but if you look closer you will see that all the ingredients of an automatic squeeze are still there.

On the play of the ace of clubs the idle king of hearts can be thrown from dummy. Since West has no hearts, the two of hearts is a sufficient one-card menace against East.

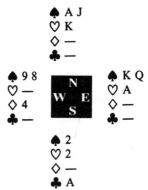

♠ A J
♡ K
◇ —
♣ —

♠ 9 8   ♠ K Q
♡ —   ♡ A
◇ 4   ◇ —
♣ —   ♣ —

♠ 2
♡ 2
◇ —
♣ A

Either or both of the menaces can be increased in length without affecting the operation of the automatic squeeze.

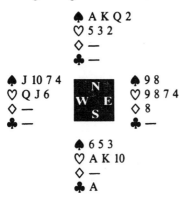

♠ A K Q 2
♡ 5 3 2
◇ —
♣ —

♠ J 10 7 4   ♠ 9 8
♡ Q J 6   ♡ 9 8 7 4
◇ —   ◇ 8
♣ —   ♣ —

♠ 6 5 3
♡ A K 10
◇ —
♣ A

On the play of the ace of clubs the defender guarding both major suits is automatically squeezed. There is no ambiguity in most automatic squeeze endings since menaces do not have to be discarded on the squeeze card. Nevertheless, in the diagram it would do no harm to cash two top spades and both top hearts before playing the squeeze card. Most players like to reduce to the simplest ending possible.

The automatic squeeze can offer an alternative line of play when a finesse seems likely to fail.

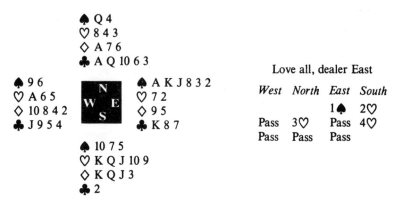

♠ Q 4
♡ 8 4 3
◇ A 7 6
♣ A Q 10 6 3

♠ 9 6   ♠ A K J 8 3 2
♡ A 6 5   ♡ 7 2
◇ 10 8 4 2   ◇ 9 5
♣ J 9 5 4   ♣ K 8 7

♠ 10 7 5
♡ K Q J 10 9
◇ K Q J 3
♣ 2

Love all, dealer East

West	North	East	South
		1♠	2♡
Pass	3♡	Pass	4♡
Pass	Pass	Pass	

West leads the nine of spades to his partner's jack. A trump comes back and your king is allowed to hold the trick. You play a spade to the queen and king and East returns his second trump. West wins and plays a third round of trumps, thereby nullifying your hopes of ruffing a spade in dummy. They are defending altogether too well. What can you do about it?

The club finesse is one way of trying for the tenth trick, or you could attempt to ruff out a doubleton king of clubs in the East hand. A third possibility is a black-suit squeeze.

The long club menace in dummy is opposite the squeeze card and the spade menace is in your own hand, so the squeeze will function automatically if East has the king of clubs. Often the choice between squeeze and finesse is a hard one, but here it is clear-cut since the bidding marks the king of clubs in the East hand.

Just play off your red winners to apply pressure. When the nine of hearts is played, East must either

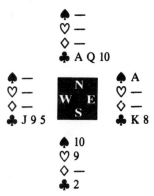

♠ —
♡ —
◇ —
♣ A Q 10

♠ —   ♠ A
♡ —   ♡ —
◇ —   ◇ —
♣ J 9 5   ♣ K 8

♠ 10
♡ 9
◇ —
♣ 2

discard the ace of spades or bare the king of clubs. Either way you make the last two tricks.

[28]

With the automatic squeeze, just as with the positional variety, you may have to do some preliminary work in order to establish a menace against a particular defender.

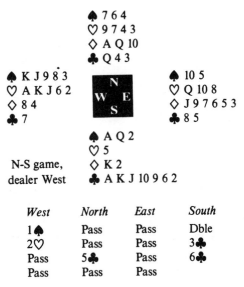

	♠ 7 6 4	
	♡ 9 7 4 3	
	◇ A Q 10	
	♣ Q 4 3	
♠ K J 9 8 3		♠ 10 5
♡ A K J 6 2		♡ Q 10 8
◇ 8 4		◇ J 9 7 6 5 3
♣ 7		♣ 8 5
	♠ A Q 2	
	♡ 5	
N-S game,	◇ K 2	
dealer West	♣ A K J 10 9 6 2	

West	North	East	South
1♠	Pass	Pass	Dble
2♡	Pass	Pass	3♣
Pass	5♣	Pass	6♣
Pass	Pass	Pass	

West leads the ace of hearts and then switches to the seven of clubs. How do you plan the play?

There are just eleven top tricks, and since the spade finesse is sure to be wrong the twelfth trick will have to come from a squeeze. The heart and spade menaces are in opposite hands so it should be possible to set up an automatic squeeze against West, but there are a couple of points to watch. First, the two-card spade menace is in your own hand, which means that the squeeze card must lie in dummy. All the trumps will have to be cashed before the diamonds, in other words. Secondly, you need two entries in dummy in order to ruff hearts and establish the nine as a menace against West alone. Since you cannot use the diamond entry until later, both of these entries must be found in the trump suit. You need the trumps to break 2–1 and you have to do a spot of unblocking.

Win the first trump with the queen and drop the six from your own hand. Ruff a heart high, cash the ace of trumps and continue with the two of trumps to dummy's four. Ruff another heart and play off the remaining trumps, discarding spades from dummy to reach this position:

Now three rounds of diamonds will make West unhappy. If both master hearts do not pop out of his hand, you will know that he has bared his king of spades.

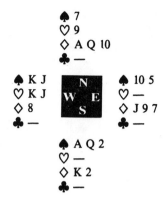

♠ 7
♡ 9
◇ A Q 10
♣ —

♠ K J   ♠ 10 5
♡ K J   ♡ —
◇ 8   ◇ J 9 7
♣ —   ♣ —

♠ A Q 2
♡ —
◇ K 2
♣ —

SPLIT TWO-CARD MENACE

In the previous chapter we saw that a split two-card menace could prove useful in a positional squeeze. This is not the case with the automatic squeeze. Except for one or two variations which will be discussed in later chapters, a split two-card menace is not only useless but positively dangerous in automatic squeeze play.

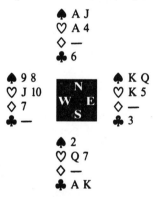

♠ A J
♡ A 4
◇ —
♣ 6

♠ 9 8   ♠ K Q
♡ J 10   ♡ K 5
◇ 7   ◇ —
♣ —   ♣ 3

♠ 2
♡ Q 7
◇ —
♣ A K

See what happens if South carelessly plays off the ace and king of clubs in this diagram. Dummy has no idle card to throw on the second club. If the four of hearts is discarded the suit is blocked, and East can escape the squeeze by baring his king of hearts.

To inflict the squeeze in this five-card ending South must first unblock by cashing the master card of the split two-card menace. After the play of the seven of hearts to the ace and a club back the menaces are suitably arranged for an automatic squeeze and the play of the last club forces East to surrender.

THE VIENNA COUP

The unblocking play mentioned above was first recorded at Vienna in the days of whist. For that reason it is known as the Vienna Coup. It is not a difficult play but it does call for a measure of foresight.

♠ K 10 7
♡ K 6
◇ A J 8 4
♣ A K Q 3

Game all, dealer West

♠ 9 8 5 2   ♠ 6
♡ Q J 9 5 4   ♡ A 8 3 2
◇ 9 3   ◇ K Q 7 2
♣ J 5   ♣ 10 9 6 4

West	North	East	South
Pass	2NT	Pass	3♠
Pass	4♣	Pass	4♠
Pass	Pass	Pass	

♠ A Q J 4 3
♡ 10 7
◇ 10 6 5
♣ 8 7 2

West leads the queen of hearts, and when dummy goes down you wish you had simply raised to three no trumps. East captures the king of hearts with his ace and returns a heart to his partner's jack. West switches to the nine of diamonds and you play low from the table. East wins with the king and returns a trump. Take it from there.

You are inclined to believe West's nine of diamonds rather than East's king. If the clubs do not break you must hope that East has the length, in which case you should be able to squeeze him in the minors. But watch it! The diamond menace is a split two-card menace and you know that is a treacherous sort of thing to have when you are contemplating an automatic squeeze.

You must employ the Vienna Coup to overcome the blockage in diamonds. After two rounds of trumps play off the diamond ace. Then finish the trumps and watch East squirm.

On the play of the last spade you throw the jack of diamonds from the table, and East has no good discard. Whether he throws the queen of diamonds or a club, you are in a position to take the rest of the tricks.

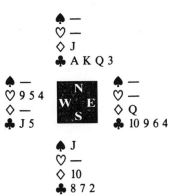

♠ —
♡ —
◇ J
♣ A K Q 3

♠ —   ♠ —
♡ 9 5 4   ♡ —
◇ —   ◇ Q
♣ J 5   ♣ 10 9 6 4

♠ J
♡ —
◇ 10
♣ 8 7 2

CHOOSING THE AUTOMATIC

When there is a choice between a positional and an automatic squeeze it is almost always right to prefer the automatic, which will work against either defender. Here is an example.

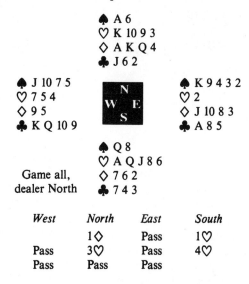

♠ A 6
♡ K 10 9 3
◇ A K Q 4
♣ J 6 2

♠ J 10 7 5
♡ 7 5 4
◇ 9 5
♣ K Q 10 9

♠ K 9 4 3 2
♡ 2
◇ J 10 8 3
♣ A 8 5

♠ Q 8
♡ A Q J 8 6
◇ 7 6 2
♣ 7 4 3

Game all,
dealer North

West	North	East	South
	1◇	Pass	1♡
Pass	3♡	Pass	4♡
Pass	Pass	Pass	

West leads the king of clubs, continues with the ten of clubs to his partner's ace, and wins the third round with the queen. You note regretfully that again three no trumps would have been a simple contract, but you have no time to dwell on this when West switches to a trump at trick four. It takes three rounds to draw the trumps, East discarding two spades. What now?

Even if the diamonds don't break there is the possibility of a spade-diamond squeeze, but in order to avoid ambiguity you need to cash the top cards in one of your menace suits before finishing the trumps. Which suit? Well, if you cash the top diamonds you will be left with a positional squeeze against West, using the split two-card menace in spades as the long menace. It must be better to play off the ace of spades, establishing the queen as a menace in your hand. Then you will have an automatic squeeze against either defender who happens to hold the king of spades and long diamonds. The ending will be as shown in the diagram.

A couple of rounds of diamonds might have been played off, but this is of no great significance. On the last heart you throw the spade from dummy, and if the king of spades does not appear you simply run the diamonds.

Now try your hand at a no trump slam.

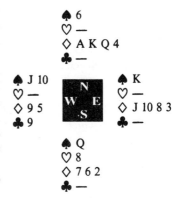

```
              ♠ 6
              ♡ —
              ◇ A K Q 4
              ♣ —
♠ J 10                      ♠ K
♡ —          N             ♡ —
◇ 9 5     W     E          ◇ J 10 8 3
♣ 9          S             ♣ —
              ♠ Q
              ♡ 8
              ◇ 7 6 2
              ♣ —
```

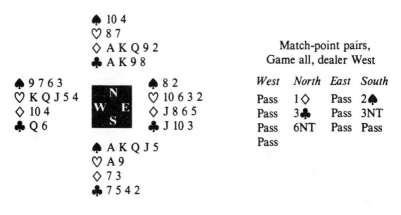

```
              ♠ 10 4
              ♡ 8 7
              ◇ A K Q 9 2
              ♣ A K 9 8
♠ 9 7 6 3                    ♠ 8 2
♡ K Q J 5 4     N           ♡ 10 6 3 2
◇ 10 4       W     E        ◇ J 8 6 5
♣ Q 6           S           ♣ J 10 3
              ♠ A K Q J 5
              ♡ A 9
              ◇ 7 3
              ♣ 7 5 4 2
```

Match-point pairs,
Game all, dealer West

West	North	East	South
Pass	1◇	Pass	2♠
Pass	3♣	Pass	3NT
Pass	6NT	Pass	Pass
Pass			

West leads the king of hearts and you see that you have a chance of making all thirteen tricks if the diamonds break evenly. Not being greedy, however, you hold off the first trick in order to rectify the count for a possible squeeze. West continues with the queen of hearts to your ace.

To prepare for the squeeze and to avoid ambiguity in the ending you should now cash the top cards in one of dummy's suits. Which one? Well, if you cash the top diamonds and run the spades, both menaces will lie in dummy and the only squeeze available will be a positional one.

You will be able to squeeze West, in other words, but not East.

Cashing the top clubs, on the other hand, will effect a double Vienna Coup, permitting you to hold the club menace in your own hand. You will then have an automatic squeeze which will succeed when *either* defender has length in the minors.

In the diagram position East has no good discard when the last spade is played.

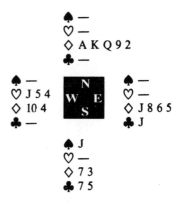

INVERSION

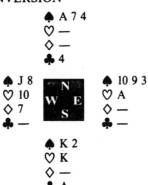

In the squeezes we have considered up to now the long menace has been in the hand opposite the squeeze card. This is the normal rule but it is not inviolable. Special types of long menace can exist in the same hand as the squeeze card, and we then have what is known as the inverted form of the automatic squeeze.

The spade menace in this diagram is called a split three-card menace. Note that in this type of menace both North and South hold master cards in the suit.

There is nothing extraordinary about the position. If the king of spades is played off, we are left with the normal form of automatic squeeze. But look what happens if we interchange the North and South club holdings.

Now the squeeze card is in the same hand as the long menace, but the inverted squeeze works just the same. This is the special property of the split three-card menace: it permits the squeeze card to lie in either hand.

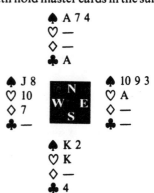

Often there will be three cards in both parts of the split three-card menace. Such menaces are common in practical play and should be preserved when you have a squeeze in mind.

A spade is discarded from dummy on the ace of clubs irrespective of the play of the defenders. In this case it is West who is squeezed out of a stopper in the majors, but it might equally well have been East.

The flexibility of the split three-card menace confers big advantages. You can accommodate the squeeze card in hand and the one-card menace on the table, or vice versa

♠ K 9 4
♡ K
♢ —
♣ —

♠ Q 7 6   ♠ J 3
♡ A   ♡ 5 3
♢ —   ♢ —
♣ —   ♣ —

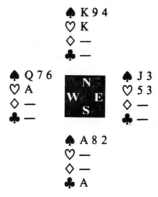

♠ A 8 2
♡ —
♢ —
♣ A

according to the needs of the situation. The versatility of the split three-card menace is illustrated on this hand.

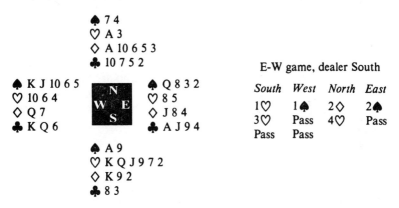

♠ 7 4
♡ A 3
♢ A 10 6 5 3
♣ 10 7 5 2

♠ K J 10 6 5
♡ 10 6 4
♢ Q 7
♣ K Q 6

♠ Q 8 3 2
♡ 8 5
♢ J 8 4
♣ A J 9 4

♠ A 9
♡ K Q J 9 7 2
♢ K 9 2
♣ 8 3

E-W game, dealer South

South	West	North	East
1♡	1♠	2♢	2♠
3♡	Pass	4♡	Pass
Pass	Pass		

West starts with the king of clubs and switches promptly to the jack of spades. How do you plan the play?

There are nine tricks in top cards, but on this defence you cannot afford to duck a diamond to develop a tenth trick. Apart from the slender chance of bringing in the diamonds without losing a trick in the suit, there is the possibility of a minor-suit squeeze. If either defender has length in both minors the squeeze will operate automatically. But you need a club ruff to isolate the club menace and you will have to be careful with the timing.

[35]

A spade must always be lost and the moment to lose it is right now, at trick two. You can win a heart switch in hand and play a club, conceding your third loser and rectifying the count for the squeeze. Winning the second heart in dummy, you ruff a club (high since you can afford it) and run the trumps to reach this position:

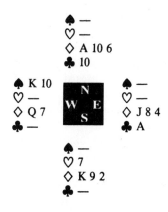

On the play of the last heart the six of diamonds is thrown from dummy and East is caught in the inverted squeeze.

The play of the last hand was not too difficult but there is always room for carelessness. Suppose you win the second trick with the ace of spades and play another club. You will escape punishment if the defenders now cash their spade, since you will simply have conceded your three tricks in a slightly different order. But the defenders have the chance to defeat you by playing a third round of clubs at trick four. When you concede the spade, a fourth round of clubs leaves you without a one-card menace in dummy and without any hope of a squeeze.

It is a frustrating hand for the defenders, who are helpless against correct play. They have to attack spades to prevent you from establishing the diamonds with a duck, and they cannot subsequently attack your diamond holding without sacrificing their trick in the suit.

THE SUBMARINE SQUEEZE

Adjusting the timing for the squeeze by rectifying the loser count is a technique that comes up time and time again. The setting may vary considerably. Usually declarer rectifies the count by refusing to win an ace immediately when the defenders attack the suit. When declarer has to take the initiative himself, underleading an honour card or even exiting with a loser in order to rectify the count, the resulting end-game is sometimes called a submarine squeeze.

```
              ♠ Q 7 6 4
              ♡ Q J 3
              ◇ 6 4 3
              ♣ 10 7 2
  ♠ J 9 5 2                 ♠ 8 3
  ♡ 10 9 8 6 2    N         ♡ A 5
  ◇ J 5        W     E      ◇ 10 9 7 2
  ♣ A 4          S          ♣ K J 9 6 5
              ♠ A K 10
              ♡ K 7 4
              ◇ A K Q 8
              ♣ Q 8 3
```

Love all, dealer North

West	North	East	South
	Pass	Pass	2NT
Pass	3NT	Pass	Pass
Pass			

West leads the ten of hearts and you count three spades, two hearts and three diamonds for a total of eight top tricks. Unless something nasty happens in the meantime you should have the chance of a ninth trick in either spades or diamonds.

Something nasty does happen. East wins the ace of hearts and switches to the club jack! That's the one card you did not wish to see. East is likely to have the club king or ace along with the nine to account for this defence. He cannot have both top clubs since he failed to open the bidding and has already produced the ace of hearts, so you play low at trick two and hope for a blockage. West follows with the four, and East continues with the six of clubs to his partner's ace. Mercifully, West switches back to hearts.

So the clubs were 5–2, that's a reprieve. East follows to the second heart and you win with the king in order to preserve an entry in dummy. You test the spades with the ace and king. Both defenders follow but no jack drops. When you continue with the ten of spades West covers with the jack, and East discards a club under dummy's queen.

Many players would see nothing to do but play on diamonds now. Those with better technique will recognise that there can be no harm in rectifying the count for a possible minor-suit squeeze by conceding the fourth spade to West, who is known to have no more clubs. South discards the queen of clubs from hand and West is on lead in the diagram position.

Whether West plays a heart now or exits with a diamond, the third round of hearts squeezes East automatically and forces him to surrender. Note that nothing would have been lost if the diamonds had been 3–3 all the time.

Something needs to be said about the defence, however. West could hardly be expected to find the initial club lead that defeats the contract out of hand, but East

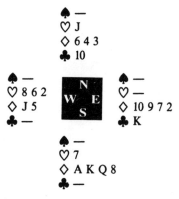

```
            ♠ —
            ♡ J
            ◇ 6 4 3
            ♣ 10
♠ —                    ♠ —
♡ 8 6 2    N           ♡ —
◇ J 5    W   E         ◇ 10 9 7 2
♣ —        S           ♣ K
            ♠ —
            ♡ 7
            ◇ A K Q 8
            ♣ —
```

was altogether too busy with his switch to the jack of clubs. If he had simply continued with a heart at trick two the declarer would have found his mission impossible.

LOSING SQUEEZE CARD

Loser-on-loser play is frequently effective in helping to rectify the count for a squeeze. In the most spectacular cases the squeeze takes place as a trick is lost to the partner of the squeezee.

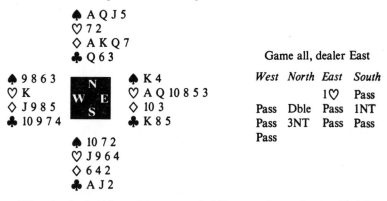

```
            ♠ A Q J 5
            ♡ 7 2
            ◇ A K Q 7
            ♣ Q 6 3
♠ 9 8 6 3              ♠ K 4
♡ K        N           ♡ A Q 10 8 5 3
◇ J 9 8 5  W   E       ◇ 10 3
♣ 10 9 7 4   S         ♣ K 8 5
            ♠ 10 7 2
            ♡ J 9 6 4
            ◇ 6 4 2
            ♣ A J 2
```

Game all, dealer East

West	North	East	South
		1♡	Pass
Pass	Dble	Pass	1NT
Pass	3NT	Pass	Pass
Pass			

West leads the king of hearts and shifts smartly to the ten of clubs. This draws the three, five and jack, and you play a low spade to the jack and king. East cashes the queen of hearts and switches back to a spade which you win with the ten.

That's annoying. East clearly does not intend to give you a ninth trick in hearts, and you will not be able to throw him in to concede two clubs at the end since you lack an entry to hand. For the moment all you can do is test the diamonds. Not unexpectedly, East discards a heart on the third round. You cash two more spades and East discards two more hearts. The position has become:

Perhaps East can be persuaded to give you a heart trick after all. When you play the seven of diamonds from dummy it acts as a losing squeeze card. East has to part with the ace of hearts or give up his club guard. This is a positional squeeze which succeeds by virtue of the fact that you, discarding after East, can keep the suit that he has unguarded. Never mind, all is grist that comes to the mill. West wins the jack of diamonds

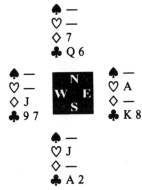

♠ —
♡ —
◇ 7
♣ Q 6

♠ —   ♠ —
♡ —   ♡ A
◇ J   ◇ —
♣ 9 7   ♣ K 8

♠ —
♡ J
◇ —
♣ A 2

and has to return a club, allowing you to make the last two tricks.

THE SUICIDE SQUEEZE

When declarer can see no possibility of rectifying the count on his own, he may still be able to persuade a defender to tighten up a squeeze position against himself. On this hand all West can do is select his method of suicide.

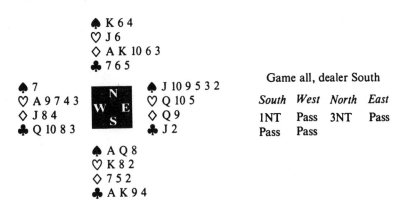

♠ K 6 4
♡ J 6
◇ A K 10 6 3
♣ 7 6 5

♠ 7   ♠ J 10 9 5 3 2
♡ A 9 7 4 3   ♡ Q 10 5
◇ J 8 4   ◇ Q 9
♣ Q 10 8 3   ♣ J 2

♠ A Q 8
♡ K 8 2
◇ 7 5 2
♣ A K 9 4

Game all, dealer South

South	West	North	East
1NT	Pass	3NT	Pass
Pass	Pass		

[39]

West leads his fourth-highest heart to the jack, queen and king. Unpleasant, isn't it? You have only eight winners, and unless you are extraordinarily lucky you will not be able to develop an extra trick in diamonds without allowing the enemy in to cash far too many hearts. The solution is to return a heart at trick two, inviting the defenders to help you rectify the count. If they run the heart suit you can discard a club and two diamonds from the table and a card in each minor from hand, coming down to the diagram position.

♠ K 6 4
♡ —
◇ A K 10
♣ 7 6

You win any return and play three rounds of spades to make West regret rectifying the count against himself.

Not that it made any difference what the defenders did. If East wins the second heart and returns, say, a club, you win and play a third heart. Now another club

♠ 7
♡ —
◇ J 8 3
♣ Q 10 8 3

♠ J 10 9 5
♡ —
◇ Q 9
♣ J 2

♠ A Q 8
♡ —
◇ 7 5
♣ A K 9

may come back, but with communications severed in both hearts and clubs you can make sure of your contract by ducking a diamond to East.

When the owner of a long suit brings pressure to bear on *himself* by cashing out, it is fitting to talk about a suicide squeeze. When he puts his *partner* on the hot spot, it is more appropriate to call it a fratricide squeeze, a homicide squeeze or even a cannibal squeeze. The notion of one defender gobbling up the other is particularly pleasing—to the declarer, at any rate.

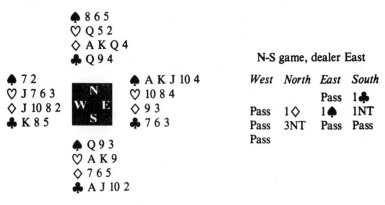

♠ 8 6 5
♡ Q 5 2
◇ A K Q 4
♣ Q 9 4

♠ 7 2
♡ J 7 6 3
◇ J 10 8 2
♣ K 8 5

♠ A K J 10 4
♡ 10 8 4
◇ 9 3
♣ 7 6 3

♠ Q 9 3
♡ A K 9
◇ 7 6 5
♣ A J 10 2

N-S game, dealer East

West	North	East	South
		Pass	1♣
Pass	1◇	1♠	1NT
Pass	3NT	Pass	Pass
Pass			

West leads the seven of spades and East puts in the ten, craftily maintaining communication with his partner. Since East passed originally you cannot hope to find him with the king of clubs. The only thing to do is to return a spade immediately, hoping that if East runs his long suit someone will get squeezed.

This is the position after the last spade. East switches to a club in response to his partner's signal, but you go up with the ace and play three rounds of hearts ending in hand.

West finds himself unable to hold the position. If the king of clubs does not pop out of his hand, you know that the diamonds must run, and you claim the rest as West reaches lovingly for his partner's throat.

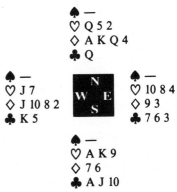

```
              ♠ —
              ♡ Q 5 2
              ♢ A K Q 4
              ♣ Q
♠ —                        ♠ —
♡ J 7        N             ♡ 10 8 4
♢ J 10 8 2  W   E          ♢ 9 3
♣ K 5          S           ♣ 7 6 3
              ♠ —
              ♡ A K 9
              ♢ 7 6
              ♣ A J 10
```

To be fair, East had no real choice but to run his spades. If he had switched after winning one, two or three spades, it would have been a simple matter for you to establish your ninth trick by finessing in clubs.

At times there can be difficulty in identifying the menaces for a squeeze.

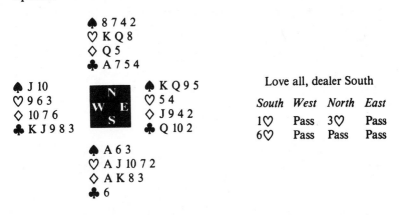

```
              ♠ 8 7 4 2
              ♡ K Q 8
              ♢ Q 5
              ♣ A 7 5 4
♠ J 10                     ♠ K Q 9 5
♡ 9 6 3      N             ♡ 5 4
♢ 10 7 6    W   E          ♢ J 9 4 2
♣ K J 9 8 3    S           ♣ Q 10 2
              ♠ A 6 3
              ♡ A J 10 7 2
              ♢ A K 8 3
              ♣ 6
```

Love all, dealer South

South	West	North	East
1♡	Pass	3♡	Pass
6♡	Pass	Pass	Pass

West leads the jack of spades and you begin to regret your impulsive bidding when dummy goes down. You appear to have just ten top tricks with five trumps, three diamonds and the two black aces. A diamond ruff in dummy could provide an eleventh trick. Where can you look for the twelfth?

Might there be a squeeze? You can hold off the first trick to rectify the count, but will this do any good? The only available menaces are in the black suits, and it is too much to hope that one defender will have four spades along with six solid clubs from the king to the eight. A club switch would break up this unlikely squeeze anyway.

If the diamond menace could be retained there might be a chance, for one defender could easily have four cards in both spades and diamonds. But there are only ten top tricks without the diamond ruff in dummy.

Instead of ruffing a diamond in dummy what about ruffing three clubs in hand? The dummy reversal will produce an eleventh trick and the diamond menace will remain intact. There may be problems with entries, but nothing else seems worth trying.

So you allow West to hold the first trick and watch anxiously for his next card. A red-suit switch will beat you by taking out an entry to dummy before you are ready to use it. But your luck is holding so far. West continues with the ten of spades and you win with the ace.

After a club to the ace, you ruff a club with the ten of hearts, play a heart to the queen, ruff another club with the jack of hearts, and play your remaining small trump. When West follows with a low card you have an awkward decision to make. You must either finesse against the nine of hearts or hope for it to drop from East, for you need a winning trump in dummy to act as your eventual squeeze card. Your decision affects the issue only when West has three hearts and East two, and the odds are therefore six to four in favour of the finesse.

You heave a sigh of relief when the finesse succeeds and East follows. The rest of the play is straightforward. Ruff the last club with the heart ace, return to dummy with the queen of diamonds and play the king of hearts, drawing West's last trump and catching East in this squeeze ending:

On the play of the king of hearts East has to abandon his guard in either spades or diamonds. With the threats divided between the North and South hands, the squeeze is automatic. It would have worked

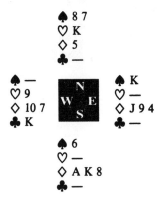

```
              ♠ 8 7
              ♡ K
              ◇ 5
              ♣ —
  ♠ —                   ♠ K
  ♡ 9      ┌───────┐    ♡ —
  ◇ 10 7   │ N     │    ◇ J 9 4
  ♣ K      │ W   E │    ♣ —
           │   S   │
           └───────┘
              ♠ 6
              ♡ —
              ◇ A K 8
              ♣ —
```

just as well against West if he had held the diamonds and the spades. On that hand the dummy reversal was the only way of releasing a menace in the long trump hand. Sometimes a partial dummy reversal is needed because there is no conceivable squeeze card opposite the long menace except a trump.

Here is an example.

♠ A K 4 3
♡ A Q 9
◇ 7 5 4
♣ Q 8 5

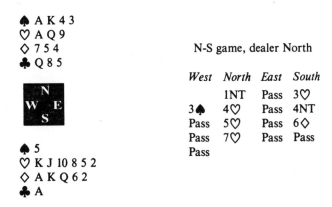

♠ 5
♡ K J 10 8 5 2
◇ A K Q 6 2
♣ A

N-S game, dealer North

West	North	East	South
	1NT	Pass	3♡
3♠	4♡	Pass	4NT
Pass	5♡	Pass	6◇
Pass	7♡	Pass	Pass
Pass			

West leads the queen of spades against your grand slam. You put on the ace and relax a little when East follows with the seven. But you can't afford to relax completely for you still have to plan the play. Any ideas?

There will be more than enough tricks on a normal 3–2 diamond break. What if the diamonds are 4–1 or 5–0? Still no problem when trumps are 2–2, for you can ruff one small diamond in dummy and discard the other on the king of spades. If East has three trumps you may well be able to set up the diamonds with one ruff in dummy. But three trumps and only one diamond with West could be a troublesome combination.

The only salvation then would be a minor-suit squeeze against East. Unfortunately the opening lead has removed the only side entry from dummy. If you run the trumps there can be no squeeze for lack of an entry in the hand opposite the squeeze card.

At first glance the problem may seem insuperable, but this is not really the case. You must simply arrange to win the last round of trumps *in dummy*. This can be done by means of a partial dummy reversal.

The key move is to ruff a small spade at trick two. Then unblock the ace of clubs and play a heart to dummy's nine. When both defenders follow suit you can continue with the dummy reversal. Ruff the small club high and play another trump to the queen. East discards a club on the second trump since the full hand is:

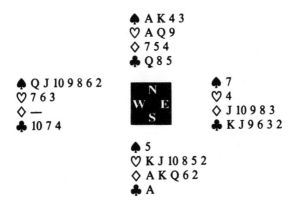

```
                  ♠ A K 4 3
                  ♡ A Q 9
                  ◇ 7 5 4
                  ♣ Q 8 5
♠ Q J 10 9 8 6 2        N        ♠ 7
♡ 7 6 3            W       E     ♡ 4
◇ —                    S         ◇ J 10 9 8 3
♣ 10 7 4                         ♣ K J 9 6 3 2
                  ♠ 5
                  ♡ K J 10 8 5 2
                  ◇ A K Q 6 2
                  ♣ A
```

Knowing the squeeze to be your only remaining chance, you ruff the last small spade in hand to reach this six-card ending.

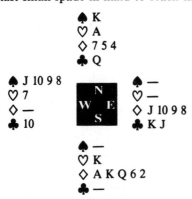

```
            ♠ K
            ♡ A
            ◇ 7 5 4
            ♣ Q
♠ J 10 9 8      N       ♠ —
♡ 7         W       E   ♡ —
◇ —             S       ◇ J 10 9 8
♣ 10                    ♣ K J
            ♠ —
            ♡ K
            ◇ A K Q 6 2
            ♣ —
```

The play of the king of hearts to dummy's ace draws the last trump, and East has an easy discard in the jack of clubs. When you continue with the spade king, however, East is automatically squeezed in the minors. No matter what discard he chooses your grand slam rolls home.

Note that the partial dummy reversal did not give you an extra trump trick. You started with six tricks in trumps and you made six tricks in trumps. What you gained by reversing the dummy was a realignment of the entry position which allowed you to win the last trump on the table. And that proved to be worth an extra trick when East was squeezed.

There are a couple of further points of interest in this hand. It underlines the advantage of playing in a good trump suit, for one thing. Twelve top tricks are always available in no trumps, but a contract of seven no trumps has no chance on a spade lead simply because declarer has no way of arranging for the squeeze card to be in dummy.

The flexibility of the trump suit overcame this problem, and it is worth noting that the more solid the suit the better when you are contemplating a dummy reversal. That is something to bear in mind when there is a choice of trump suits.

4

Overcoming a Blockage

A point brought out in the first chapter was that the long menace must lie in the hand opposite the squeeze card. That is the general rule, but like most of the rules of squeeze play it has plenty of exceptions. We have already met one of those exceptions—the inverted squeeze where the long menace lies in the same hand as the squeeze card. The inverted squeeze works because there is adequate compensation in the form of a master card of the long menace suit in the hand opposite the squeeze card. There must always be some compensating factor to enable a squeeze to function when the entries and menaces are arranged in an irregular way.

THE CRISS-CROSS SQUEEZE

As we have already noted, a split two-card menace is normally of no value in an automatic squeeze. But there is one particular case in which it can be effective. That is where there are split two-card menaces in two suits with one master card in each hand. This arrangement permits a third form of automatic squeeze—the criss-cross squeeze—to exist. Its frequency of occurrence is not as great as that of the normal automatic or even the inverted squeeze. Nevertheless it can be useful when it does turn ''p and it is important to be able to recognise this variation.

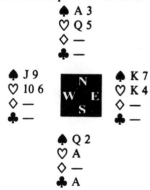

In this diagram there are split two-card menaces in both major suits. North holds the master card in South's suit while South has the master card in North's suit.

When the ace of clubs is played

the small spade is thrown from dummy and East is automatically squeezed. South next cashes the ace of whichever suit East has unguarded, and the other ace gives access to the established winner. The squeeze would work equally well against West if he had the guarded kings in the majors.

Perhaps you have noticed the undesirable feature of the criss-cross squeeze. After the squeeze card has been played you still have master cards in both menace suits, and this means that unless you have a complete count of the hand you may have difficulty in deciding which suit the defender has unguarded at the end. If East had blanked one of his kings at an earlier stage he might have persuaded you to cash the major suit aces in the wrong order.

The usual way to avoid this kind of ambiguity is to play off all the top cards in one of the menace suits before playing the squeeze card, but for technical reasons this is not possible with the criss-cross squeeze. If the ace of hearts is cashed before the ace of clubs in the above diagram only a positional squeeze remains, while if the ace of spades is cashed first you are left with no squeeze at all.

The criss-cross squeeze is one of a large group of squeezes in which ambiguity is often inherent and can be overcome only by accurate card-reading.

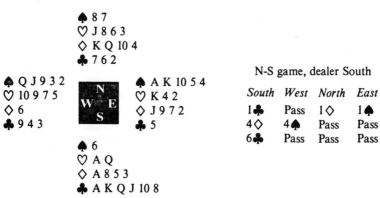

♠ 8 7
♡ J 8 6 3
◇ K Q 10 4
♣ 7 6 2

♠ Q J 9 3 2   ♠ A K 10 5 4
♡ 10 9 7 5   ♡ K 4 2
◇ 6   ◇ J 9 7 2
♣ 9 4 3   ♣ 5

♠ 6
♡ A Q
◇ A 8 5 3
♣ A K Q J 10 8

N-S game, dealer South

South	West	North	East
1♣	Pass	1◇	1♠
4◇	4♠	Pass	Pass
6♣	Pass	Pass	Pass

West leads the queen of spades and continues with a low spade to his partner's king. You ruff, draw trumps in three rounds, play a diamond to the queen and finesse the queen of hearts successfully.

East is marked with the king of hearts and you still have a split three-card menace in diamonds. You can therefore cash the heart ace and run the rest of the trumps to catch East in an inverted automatic squeeze.

On the play of the ten of clubs in the diagram position you throw a diamond from dummy, and East has to abandon one of the red suits.

Although crowned with success, this would be a sad and bad way to play the hand. The inverted squeeze

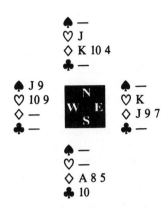

works because East has the diamond length, but there is no good reason why East should not hold a singleton diamond along with extra length in the majors. Correct play guarantees the contract no matter

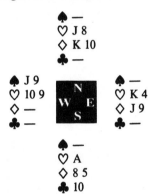

who has the diamond length. Keep the ace of hearts in hand and cash the ace of diamonds instead. If East shows out, you have a marked finesse for the contract. When in practice West shows out on the second round of diamonds, you just run the remaining trumps to squeeze East by the criss-cross method.

The ten of diamonds is discarded on your last trump and East is unable to withstand the pressure.

No ambiguity arises in this particular case because you have a count of the diamonds.

In the next hand the position is subtly different.

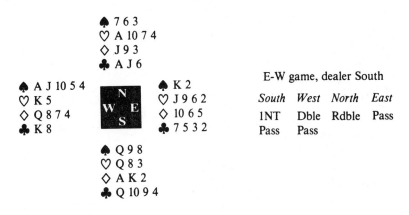

♠ 7 6 3
♡ A 10 7 4
◇ J 9 3
♣ A J 6

♠ A J 10 5 4
♡ K 5
◇ Q 8 7 4
♣ K 8

♠ K 2
♡ J 9 6 2
◇ 10 6 5
♣ 7 5 3 2

♠ Q 9 8
♡ Q 8 3
◇ A K 2
♣ Q 10 9 4

E-W game, dealer South

South	West	North	East
1NT	Dble	Rdble	Pass
Pass	Pass		

West doubles your weak no trump but runs into a redouble. In view of the vulnerability he decides to take his medicine by passing.

The lead of the jack of spades goes to the king and the defenders take the first five tricks. You discard two hearts from dummy and a heart and a diamond from your own hand, while East discards three clubs. West exits with the eight of clubs which runs to your nine. The king of clubs appears on the second round as East discards a diamond. You play a diamond to your king and cash the queen of clubs, on which both defenders throw small hearts. The position is as shown in the diagram.

♠ —
♡ A 10
◇ J 9
♣ —

♠ —
♡ Q 8
◇ A
♣ 10

On the last club you can throw the ten of hearts from dummy, and if either defender controls both red suits he will be caught in a criss-cross squeeze.

But what is this nonsense about 'either defender?' You know from the bidding who holds the stoppers and you have no need of an automatic squeeze. There is no sense in playing a criss-cross just because the requirements are there. It is a positional squeeze that will serve you best in this case. Cash the ace of diamonds before the last club to remove all ambiguity from the ending.

When the diamond queen does not appear at trick eleven, you realise that West must have bared the king of hearts earlier, and the way to make an overtrick is clear.

A slightly different form of criss-cross squeeze can develop when declarer threatens to make *two* extra tricks in one of the menace suits.

Here is an example.

```
              ♠ —
              ♡ A 10
              ◇ J
              ♣ —
♠ —          N          ♠ —
♡ K      W       E      ♡ J 9 6
◇ Q 8        S          ◇ —
♣ —                     ♣ —
              ♠ —
              ♡ Q 8
              ◇ —
              ♣ 10
```

```
              ♠ A 8 7 4
              ♡ J 10 5
              ◇ A K 3
              ♣ K 6 4
♠ 9 6 5       N          ♠ Q 10 3 2
♡ 8 4     W       E      ♡ A 7 2
◇ 9 4 2       S          ◇ Q 8 6
♣ Q J 9 7 3              ♣ A 10 5
              ♠ K J
              ♡ K Q 9 6 3
              ◇ J 10 7 5
              ♣ 8 2
```

Love all, dealer East

West	North	East	South
		1NT	Pass
Pass	Dble	Pass	Pass
2♣	Pass	Pass	3♡
Pass	4♡	Pass	Pass
Pass			

West leads the queen of clubs and continues with the jack of clubs to the king and ace. East perseveres with the ten of clubs which you ruff in hand. The king of hearts is allowed to win the next trick, but East takes his ace on the second round and returns a third heart to dummy's jack. How do you continue?

East is marked with the queens of both spades and diamonds, so you should play a spade for a finesse of the jack and then play off the last trump, discarding the small diamond from the table. You have to hope that East began with four cards in spades. It is an irregular sort of criss-

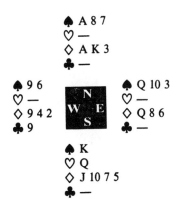

♠ A 8 7
♡ —
◇ A K 3
♣ —

♠ 9 6   ♠ Q 10 3
♡ —   ♡ —
◇ 9 4 2   ◇ Q 8 6
♣ 9   ♣ —

♠ K
♡ Q
◇ J 10 7 5
♣ —

cross since you have a blocked spade position with winners in both hands. But the extra length in diamonds provides sufficient compensation.

If East discards a diamond on the queen of hearts, you will make only two spade tricks but you will score two extra tricks in diamonds.

It is worth noting that East could have defeated this squeeze by returning a spade at trick three and a further spade when he gained the lead with the ace of hearts.

RESCUE MANOEUVRES

Many squeezes with irregular entry positions occur when declarer has the high cards to win all the remaining tricks but is thwarted by a blockage in dummy.

Here the long menace is in the same hand as the squeeze card but that doesn't comfort West one bit. On the play of the ace of clubs he is obliged to unguard one of the majors. If he lets go the heart ace, South continues with the ten of spades to dummy's king and enjoys the heart king. If West parts with a spade South plays the ace of spades next, crashing the outstanding honour card and promoting his ten.

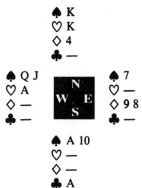

♠ K
♡ K
◇ 4
♣ —

♠ Q J   ♠ 7
♡ A   ♡ —
◇ —   ◇ 9 8
♣ —   ♣ —

♠ A 10
♡ —
◇ —
♣ A

The fact that North's king of spades is of master rank is sufficient compensation for the unorthodox lie of the menaces. If declarer had been able to unblock in spades at an earlier stage no squeeze would have been necessary. All the squeeze does, in fact, is to restore to declarer the tricks that are rightfully his. Blocked squeezes of this sort are always automatic, working equally well against either defender.

Not much variation is possible, but the one-card menace may be accompanied by a winner provided that the long menace is also extended.

In this diagram dummy's diamond is discarded on the ace of clubs and East finds himself unable to cope.

While not exactly common, these blocked squeezes do make an occasional appearance. In a suit contract it may be inadvisable to unblock because of the danger of an enemy ruff. And we sometimes find ourselves playing a no-trump game where the communications are especially difficult.

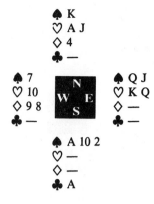

    ♠ K
    ♡ A J
    ◇ 4
    ♣ —
♠ 7   ♠ Q J
♡ 10   ♡ K Q
◇ 9 8   ◇ —
♣ —   ♣ —
    ♠ A 10 2
    ♡ —
    ◇ —
    ♣ A

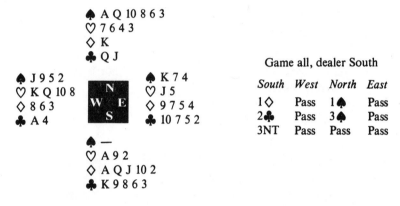

                    ♠ A Q 10 8 6 3
                    ♡ 7 6 4 3
                    ◇ K
                    ♣ Q J
    ♠ J 9 5 2   ♠ K 7 4
    ♡ K Q 10 8   ♡ J 5
    ◇ 8 6 3   ◇ 9 7 5 4
    ♣ A 4   ♣ 10 7 5 2
                    ♠ —
                    ♡ A 9 2
                    ◇ A Q J 10 2
                    ♣ K 9 8 6 3

Game all, dealer South

South	West	North	East
1◇	Pass	1♠	Pass
2♣	Pass	3♠	Pass
3NT	Pass	Pass	Pass

West leads the king of hearts on which East drops the jack. You hold off the first trick but win the heart continuation and play a club. West goes up with the ace and cashes his two hearts, East discarding diamonds while you part with a club. West then exits in the only suit to cause you difficulty—diamonds.

At first glance it may seem that you need to find the ten of clubs doubleton, but there is a good auxiliary chance. You should overtake the king of diamonds with your ace and run the suit, discarding spades from dummy. If either defender holds the ten of clubs along with the king of spades he will be caught in the extended version of the blocked squeeze.

On the play of the last diamond you throw the ten of spades from dummy. East has to unguard one of the black suits, enabling you to make the rest of the tricks in one hand or the other.

Since you had to retain top cards in both menace suits ambiguity was unavoidable. East might have misled you by better discarding— blanking the spade king earlier, for instance.

Now try your hand at a slam.

♠ A Q 10
♡ —
◇ —
♣ Q

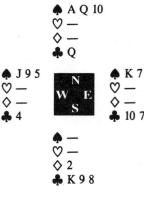

♠ J 9 5   ♠ K 7
♡ —   ♡ —
◇ —   ◇ —
♣ 4   ♣ 10 7

♠ —
♡ —
◇ 2
♣ K 9 8

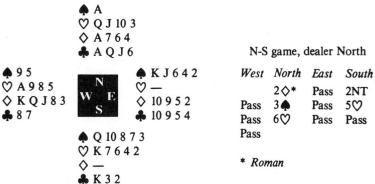

♠ A
♡ Q J 10 3
◇ A 7 6 4
♣ A Q J 6

♠ 9 5   ♠ K J 6 4 2
♡ A 9 8 5   ♡ —
◇ K Q J 8 3   ◇ 10 9 5 2
♣ 8 7   ♣ 10 9 5 4

♠ Q 10 8 7 3
♡ K 7 6 4 2
◇ —
♣ K 3 2

N-S game, dealer North

West	North	East	South
	2◇*	Pass	2NT
Pass	3♠	Pass	5♡
Pass	6♡	Pass	Pass
Pass			

* *Roman*

West leads the king of diamonds. You play low from dummy, ruff in hand and play a small trump to the ten, receiving a rude shock when East shows out. There is nothing for it but to continue on reverse dummy lines. Ruff another diamond, play a club to dummy's jack and ruff the remaining small diamond. But when you play your last trump, the king, West still declines to take his ace.

This creates a bit of a problem in communications. You cannot afford to enter dummy with the ace of spades, since that would allow West to force you with a second spade when he is in with the ace of hearts. Nor would it be safe to play the king and another club, for West might score a ruff with his small trump. It goes against the grain to block the club suit by playing your small club to dummy's queen on the second round, but this does appear to be the safest way of entering dummy.

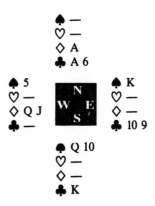

♠ —
♡ —
◇ A
♣ A 6

♠ Q 10
♡ —
◇ —
♣ K

When the queen of clubs scores, you continue with the heart queen from the table. West wins and unsportingly returns a spade to the ace, setting the seal on the club blockage. But there is no need to despair even if the clubs are breaking 4–2. Draw the last trump and continue with the ace of diamonds. East, if he has the king of spades along with length in clubs, will be unable to withstand the pressure.

No ambiguity arises in this case, of course. If the king of spades does not pop out for all to see, your next play will be the ace of clubs.

THE JETTISON SQUEEZE

Suppose, in the last hand, that you had won the second round of clubs with the ace instead of with the queen. The ending would have been as shown in the new diagram.

The squeeze still works! The only difference is that if East parts with a club on the play of the ace of diamonds you have to jettison the club king from your hand.

This jettison squeeze, where the blocking singleton is the highest-ranking card in the suit, is quite rare. If you manage to recognise and execute such a squeeze you should be able to dine out on it for some time.

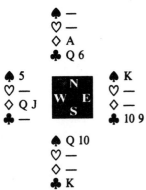

♠ —
♡ —
◇ A
♣ Q 6

♠ Q 10
♡ —
◇ —
♣ K

Your discard in the hand opposite the squeeze card depends on the discard of the defender, which means that the jettison squeeze is a positional one, playable only against the defender on the left of the squeeze card. Clearly on a hand like the last one where there was a choice between the normal blocked squeeze and the jettison squeeze, one should opt for the automatic ending.

But sometimes the jettison squeeze is the only one available.

♠ Q 6 3
♡ A K Q
♢ J 10 8 4 3
♣ Q J

Love all, dealer West

♠ 7 2　　　　　♠ 9 8 5
♡ 9 8 6 2　　　♡ J 5
♢ A K Q 7 5　　♢ 9 6 2
♣ A 7　　　　　♣ 10 9 6 5 2

West	North	East	South
1♢	1NT	Pass	3♠
Pass	4♡	Pass	5♢
Pass	5♡	Pass	6♠
Pass	Pass	Pass	

♠ A K J 10 4
♡ 10 7 4 3
♢ —
♣ K 8 4 3

West leads the ace of diamonds for you to ruff. When you play a small club West goes up with the ace and forces you again with the king of diamonds.

After ruffing you are down to three trumps, and the entry position is critical because of the blockages in hearts and clubs. It looks right to test the hearts next since you appear to need a 3–3 break in the suit. East drops the jack on the second round, however, and you have to think again.

That jack of hearts does not necessarily mean that the hearts are breaking 4–2, but it would be wise to take account of the possibility. If West has length in hearts along with his marked queen of diamonds, he will surely be in some difficulty when you run your winners. You should therefore cash the queen of clubs, return to hand with a trump, ruff the small club on the table with the queen of spades, and play out the remaining trumps, which you need to find 3–2.

When you play the king of clubs in the diagram position, West is caught in the net of the jettison squeeze. Unless he discards the queen of diamonds, you ditch the queen of hearts from dummy and take the last two tricks with ♡ 10 and ♡ 7.

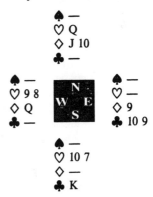

♠ —
♡ Q
♢ J 10
♣ —

♠ —　　　　♠ —
♡ 9 8　　　♡ —
♢ Q　　　　♢ 9
♣ —　　　　♣ 10 9

♠ —
♡ 10 7
♢ —
♣ K

Note that this play still succeeds in the case where the hearts are 3–3 all the time.

5

The Ruffing Squeeze

In the squeezes we have examined up to now the trump suit has sometimes played a limited role. Trumps have been used for ruffing out stoppers and isolating menaces, and often the squeeze card itself has been a trump.

In what is called the ruffing squeeze, however, trumps have an important part to play *after* the squeeze has taken effect. The most common type of ruffing squeeze uses the split two-card menace as the long menace. Consider this diagram.

There is a split two-card menace in hearts and a ruffing menace in spades. The ruffing menace is just an extended one-card menace— that is to say, a one-card menace accompanied by an extra card in the suit. This makes it necessary for the defender to keep a guard to his stopper lest it be ruffed out.

But when South plays a club to the ace in the above position, East is helpless. He must either blank the

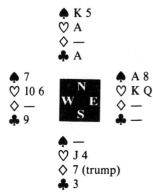

ace of spades, which allows it to be ruffed away, or discard one of his heart honours. In the latter case declarer cashes the heart ace and enters hand with a spade ruff to enjoy the established jack of hearts.

Note the close similarity between this squeeze and one of those we studied in the last chapter—the criss-cross squeeze. The only difference is that in the ruffing squeeze declarer does not hold a master card in dummy's suit but instead uses a ruff to return to hand. As one would expect, the ruffing squeeze suffers from the same disadvantage as the criss-cross squeeze. Ambiguity is likely to be present unless declarer has a count on one of the vital suits.

In most squeezes the damage is inflicted by the lead of the declarer's last free winner—that is the last winner in the suits not involved in the squeeze. In the ruffing squeeze, however, the squeeze card is the *second last* free winner; there is always a trump left in declarer's hand after the squeeze has taken effect. This is made possible by the fact that the defender has an extra burden to carry. He needs to try to hold on to an extra 'busy' card—the guard that prevents his winner from being ruffed out.

In the ruffing squeeze there must always be two cards of entry in the hand containing the ruffing menace, one to establish the menace and the other to cash it. One of these entries is the master card of the split two-card menace; the other may lie in any of the four suits. When the second entry is in the free side suit as in the

diagram on the previous page, or in trumps as in this diagram, it will also be the squeeze card.

South plays a trump to dummy's ten and East feels the pinch as before. Whether he parts with a heart or a spade, declarer takes the rest of the tricks.

Ruffing squeezes merit serious study, although they are not met with every day. It is a great ad-vantage to be able to recognise the

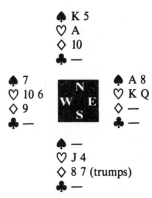

♠ K 5
♡ A
◇ 10
♣ —

♠ 7   ♠ A 8
♡ 10 6   ♡ K Q
◇ 9   ◇ —
♣ —   ♣ —

♠ —
♡ J 4
◇ 8 7 (trumps)
♣ —

possibilities when you come across a hand like the following.

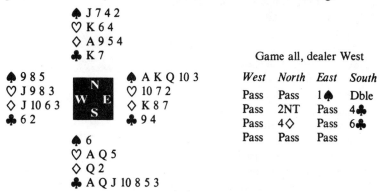

♠ J 7 4 2
♡ K 6 4
◇ A 9 5 4
♣ K 7

♠ 9 8 5   ♠ A K Q 10 3
♡ J 9 8 3   ♡ 10 7 2
◇ J 10 6 3   ◇ K 8 7
♣ 6 2   ♣ 9 4

♠ 6
♡ A Q 5
◇ Q 2
♣ A Q J 10 8 5 3

Game all, dealer West

West	North	East	South
Pass	Pass	1♠	Dble
Pass	2NT	Pass	4♣
Pass	4◇	Pass	6♣
Pass	Pass	Pass	

It is lucky for you that East did not see fit to double four diamonds, for a diamond lead would have left you with no chance. West leads the nine of spades and you cover with the jack because you fear a diamond switch. East wins with the queen and shifts to the seven of hearts.

You can count no more than eleven tricks. The twelfth will need to come from a spade-diamond squeeze, but the only long menace is the split two-card menace in diamonds and you know that to be useless for automatic squeeze purposes. The ruffing squeeze ought to work, however. Win the heart in hand with the ace, cross to the king of clubs and ruff a spade high. Run four more trumps discarding diamonds from dummy, and cash the queen of hearts. Then play a heart to the king to inflict the squeeze in the diagram position.

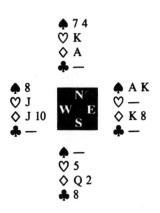

♠ 7 4
♡ K
♢ A
♣ —

♠ 8
♡ J
♢ J 10
♣ —

♠ A K
♡ —
♢ K 8
♣ —

♠ —
♡ 5
♢ Q 2
♣ 8

East has to weaken his holding in one suit or the other, and you establish your twelfth trick in the suit of his discard.

When the squeeze card is with the long trumps, the second entry to the other hand must be in one of the menace suits.

Here the squeeze card is the ten of diamonds, but North has an additional master card in the suit of the split two-card menace, and the squeeze functions satisfactorily when the two of hearts is discarded from the table.

Most ruffing squeezes are automatic, working equally well against either opponent. But in practice the squeeze is of value mainly against the opponent on the right of the trumps. A ruffing squeeze against

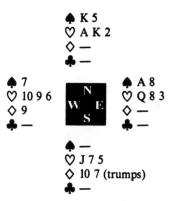

♠ K 5
♡ A K 2
♢ —
♣ —

♠ 7
♡ 10 9 6
♢ 9
♣ —

♠ A 8
♡ Q 8 3
♢ —
♣ —

♠ —
♡ J 7 5
♢ 10 7 (trumps)
♣ —

the other opponent is not often needed. In the above diagram if the East and West cards are transposed, for example, all South need do is play out both trumps to squeeze West positionally.

When the split two-card menace is blocked from the start, however, a ruffing squeeze may be needed against the lefthand opponent. Here is an example.

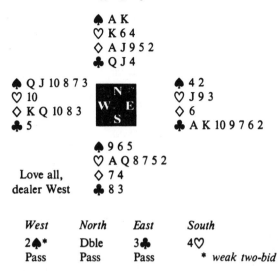

♠ A K
♡ K 6 4
◇ A J 9 5 2
♣ Q J 4

♠ Q J 10 8 7 3   ♠ 4 2
♡ 10   ♡ J 9 3
◇ K Q 10 8 3   ◇ 6
♣ 5   ♣ A K 10 9 7 6 2

♠ 9 6 5
♡ A Q 8 7 5 2
Love all,   ◇ 7 4
dealer West   ♣ 8 3

West	North	East	South
2♠*	Dble	3♣	4♡
Pass	Pass	Pass	* weak two-bid

West led his singleton club to the jack and king. East continued with the ace and another club, South discarding a diamond as West ruffed with the ten of hearts. The ace of diamonds was knocked out at trick four and South was faced with the task of making the rest of the tricks. He tested the trumps with the king and saw West show out There could be no point in trying to ruff the third spade in dummy since East would be able to over-ruff. But the situation was far from hopeless. South ruffed a diamond and drew the remaining trumps, leaving this position:

When the eight of hearts was played West was stuck for a discard. There was no possibility of deception since declarer had a complete count. If West had thrown a diamond, South would have crossed to the king of spades, ruffed out West's last diamond, and returned to dummy with the spade ace to score the diamond jack.

When in practice West discarded a spade, South played off the top spades and ruffed himself back to hand to enjoy the nine of spades.

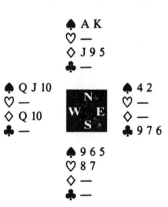

♠ A K
♡ —
◇ J 9 5
♣ —

♠ Q J 10   ♠ 4 2
♡ —   ♡ —
◇ Q 10   ◇ —
♣ —   ♣ 9 7 6

♠ 9 6 5
♡ 8 7
◇ —
♣ —

The second entry to the hand opposite the trumps may also lie in the suit of the ruffing menace, as is shown in the next diagram.

Dummy's three of hearts goes on the ten of diamonds and East wilts under the pressure.

For a genuine ruffing squeeze to exist in this situation it is necessary for West to control the second round of spades. Otherwise the declarer could have reduced the position to an automatic squeeze against East by playing off the ace of hearts at an earlier stage.

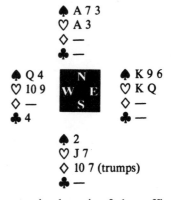

♠ A 7 3
♡ A 3
♢ —
♣ —

♠ Q 4   ♠ K 9 6
♡ 10 9   ♡ K Q
♢ —   ♢ —
♣ 4   ♣ —

♠ 2
♡ J 7
♢ 10 7 (trumps)
♣ —

Quite frequently you will find an entry in the suit of the ruffing menace and the position is worth remembering.

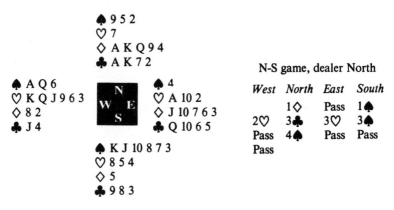

♠ 9 5 2
♡ 7
♢ A K Q 9 4
♣ A K 7 2

♠ A Q 6   ♠ 4
♡ K Q J 9 6 3   ♡ A 10 2
♢ 8 2   ♢ J 10 7 6 3
♣ J 4   ♣ Q 10 6 5

♠ K J 10 8 7 3
♡ 8 5 4
♢ 5
♣ 9 8 3

N-S game, dealer North

West	North	East	South
	1♢	Pass	1♠
2♡	3♣	3♡	3♠
Pass	4♠	Pass	Pass
Pass			

West leads the king of hearts and East overtakes with the ace in order to return a trump. When you play low, West takes his queen of spades and continues with the ace and another, denying you any chance of ruffing a heart in dummy.

It will be a simple matter to establish a tenth trick if the diamonds are 4–3, but East could well have length in the minor suits. What are the squeeze prospects? If it were possible to play off the top clubs and get back to hand without destroying the diamond entry, you might have an automatic 'squeeze against East. Poor communications make it impossible, but this is just the sort of situation where the ruffing squeeze can come to your aid. Play off another couple of trumps, discarding small clubs from dummy.

On the jack of spades you throw the seven of clubs from the table and East is caught in the familiar, painful dilemma.

There is no ambiguity since you will have a count of the diamonds after three rounds.

Many players would have gone wrong on this hand by playing diamonds too soon, not appreciating the advantage of putting the idle trumps to work first.

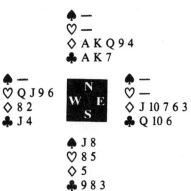

```
                ♠ —
                ♡ —
                ◇ A K Q 9 4
                ♣ A K 7
♠ —                              ♠ —
♡ Q J 9 6        N               ♡ —
◇ 8 2         W     E            ◇ J 10 7 6 3
♣ J 4            S               ♣ Q 10 6
                ♠ J 8
                ♡ 8 5
                ◇ 5
                ♣ 9 8 3
```

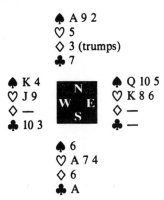

```
                ♠ A 9 2
                ♡ 5
                ◇ 3 (trumps)
                ♣ 7
♠ K 4                            ♠ Q 10 5
♡ J 9            N               ♡ K 8 6
◇ —          W     E            ◇ —
♣ 10 3           S               ♣ —
                ♠ 6
                ♡ A 7 4
                ◇ 6
                ♣ A
```

South will make all six tricks.

The squeeze is automatic and the squeeze card may lie in either hand. In practice the above position can be simplified, for it is not necessary to have a winner accompanying the ruffing menace that lies in the same hand as the squeeze card.

The ace of hearts has been played off without detracting from the potency of the squeeze, but now the

There is another important type of ruffing squeeze that does not require a split two-card menace. It makes use of two ruffing menaces instead. The ruffing menaces are divided and there are trumps in both hands.

South has five immediate winners —the three aces plus a trump in each hand. If either defender has sole control of the third round of both major suits, he will be squeezed on the play of the ace of clubs and

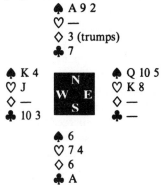

```
                ♠ A 9 2
                ♡ —
                ◇ 3 (trumps)
                ♣ 7
♠ K 4                            ♠ Q 10 5
♡ J              N               ♡ K 8
◇ —          W     E            ◇ —
♣ 10 3           S               ♣ —
                ♠ 6
                ♡ 7 4
                ◇ 6
                ♣ A
```

squeeze card must lie in the South hand. There must always be some means of access to the ruffing menace that lies opposite the squeeze card.

This type of ruffing squeeze should be considered when it seems unlikely that effective menaces are present for an ordinary positional or automatic squeeze.

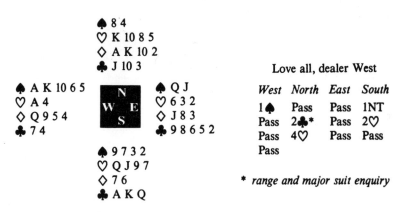

♠ 8 4
♡ K 10 8 5
♢ A K 10 2
♣ J 10 3

♠ A K 10 6 5
♡ A 4
♢ Q 9 5 4
♣ 7 4

♠ Q J
♡ 6 3 2
♢ J 8 3
♣ 9 8 6 5 2

♠ 9 7 3 2
♡ Q J 9 7
♢ 7 6
♣ A K Q

Love all, dealer West

West	North	East	South
1♠	Pass	Pass	1NT
Pass	2♣*	Pass	2♡
Pass	4♡	Pass	Pass
Pass			

* *range and major suit enquiry*

West leads the ace of spades on which East plays the queen. Annoyingly, West switches to the ace and another heart. You win in hand and play a second spade, but East wins with the jack and plays a third trump on which West discards a spade.

The defenders have denied you the chance of ruffing two spades in dummy or two diamonds in hand, but you still have some chances for the contract. One possibility is to bank on West having both diamond honours. You would not actually need to take the double finesse. West is marked with five spades, so you could just ruff a spade in dummy, cash the clubs and continue with the last trump to effect a simple squeeze.

But the ruffing squeeze gives a better chance, succeeding not only when West has both diamond honours but when he has any four diamonds. Just play off the clubs to apply pressure.

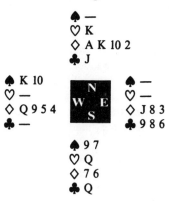

♠ —
♡ K
♢ A K 10 2
♣ J

♠ K 10
♡ —
♢ Q 9 5 4
♣ —

♠ —
♡ —
♢ J 8 3
♣ 9 8 6

♠ 9 7
♡ Q
♢ 7 6
♣ Q

When the last club is played West can no longer hold the position. Whether he discards a spade or a diamond, you can ruff out the suit of his discard to create a tenth trick for yourself.

When you have two ruffing menaces it is usually right to aim for a balanced trump position with an equal number of trumps in each hand. Some early ruffs may be needed to achieve this balance before the squeeze card is played.

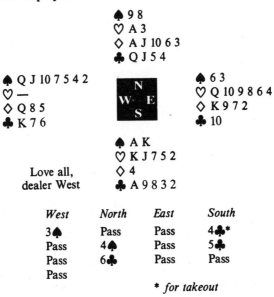

```
                    ♠ 9 8
                    ♡ A 3
                    ◇ A J 10 6 3
                    ♣ Q J 5 4
♠ Q J 10 7 5 4 2          N          ♠ 6 3
♡ —                   W     E        ♡ Q 10 9 8 6 4
◇ Q 8 5                   S          ◇ K 9 7 2
♣ K 7 6                              ♣ 10
                    ♠ A K
                    ♡ K J 7 5 2
   Love all,        ◇ 4
   dealer West      ♣ A 9 8 3 2
```

West	North	East	South
3♠	Pass	Pass	4♣*
Pass	4♠	Pass	5♣
Pass	6♣	Pass	Pass
Pass			

* for takeout

Winning the spade lead with the king, you cross to the ace of diamonds and run the queen of clubs. West produces the king and returns a club, which you win in hand as East discards a spade. You draw the remaining trump with the jack of clubs, East discarding a heart. What now?

West is marked with ten cards in the black suits and East with ten in the reds. You can be pretty sure that the heart finesse is working, and you should be able to squeeze East in the red suits for your twelfth trick. The squeeze card will be the ace of spades, but it would be premature to play the nine of spades to your ace at this point. The position is as shown in the diagram overleaf:

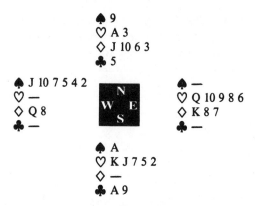

```
              ♠ 9
              ♡ A 3
              ◇ J 10 6 3
              ♣ 5
♠ J 10 7 5 4 2            ♠ —
♡ —             N        ♡ Q 10 9 8 6
◇ Q 8        W   E       ◇ K 8 7
♣ —             S        ♣ —
              ♠ A
              ♡ K J 7 5 2
              ◇ —
              ♣ A 9
```

First you must ruff a diamond in hand. This serves the dual purpose of helping to count the hand and balancing the trump position for the ruffing squeeze. The play of the ace of spades will then grind East into the dust.

If East parts with another heart, you can set up your fifth heart with the help of a finesse against the queen and a ruff in dummy. If East throws a diamond, one further diamond ruff suffices to set up the suit and you no longer need the heart finesse.

In this case the squeeze card was in your own hand and there was no diamond entry to dummy. But the ace of hearts and the extra diamond length provided adequate compensation and the squeeze worked like a charm.

There was a hand in the World Pairs Olympiad at Stockholm where a slam could be made with no more than half the high cards in the pack.

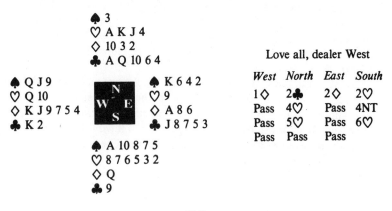

```
              ♠ 3
              ♡ A K J 4
              ◇ 10 3 2
              ♣ A Q 10 6 4       Love all, dealer West
♠ Q J 9                  ♠ K 6 4 2
♡ Q 10          N        ♡ 9
◇ K J 9 7 5 4  W   E     ◇ A 8 6
♣ K 2           S        ♣ J 8 7 5 3
              ♠ A 10 8 7 5
              ♡ 8 7 6 5 3 2
              ◇ Q
              ♣ 9
```

West	North	East	South
1◇	2♣	2◇	2♡
Pass	4♡	Pass	4NT
Pass	5♡	Pass	6♡
Pass	Pass	Pass	

From the bidding it appears that you were desperate for points. Well, you have a chance to earn them here. West leads the seven of diamonds to his partner's ace and you ruff the diamond return. Trumps are drawn with the ace and king, East discarding his remaining diamond on the second round. How do you continue?

Eight trumps and two black aces give you a total of ten tricks. An eleventh could come from a successful club finesse and a twelfth from setting up a long club. But there is also the chance of a black suit squeeze against East who, to judge from his discards, is very likely to have

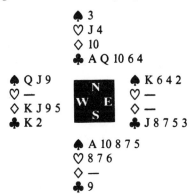

started with four spades and five clubs. In that case the club finesse will not be necessary. To bring pressure to bear you should ruff dummy's third diamond at this point.

If East discards a club when the ten of diamonds is played, you can continue with a club to the ace and a club ruff. If instead he discards a spade, you can establish the spades with two ruffs in dummy.

♠ 3
♡ J 4
◇ 10
♣ A Q 10 6 4

♠ Q J 9   ♠ K 6 4 2
♡ —   ♡ —
◇ K J 9 5   ◇ —
♣ K 2   ♣ J 8 7 5 3

♠ A 10 8 7 5
♡ 8 7 6
◇ —
♣ 9

In that hand the squeeze card was a trump used to ruff a card in a side suit. A trump that is led can also act as the squeeze card in this type of ruffing squeeze. Obviously there must be an outstanding trump that needs to be drawn. Otherwise you would simply play a cross-ruff.

The play of the ten of diamonds draws West's trump and squeezes East at the same time. No matter what East discards, you can establish an extra trick in the suit of the discard to bring in the rest of the tricks.

If West's trump had been of lowly rank, you might have been able to make the rest of the tricks on a cross-ruff anyway. The ruffing squeeze allows you to overcome the relatively high rank of West's bothersome trump.

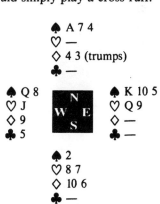

♠ A 7 4
♡ —
◇ 4 3 (trumps)
♣ —

♠ Q 8   ♠ K 10 5
♡ J   ♡ Q 9
◇ 9   ◇ —
♣ 5   ♣ —

♠ 2
♡ 8 7
◇ 10 6
♣ —

Particularly fascinating is the positional version of this ruffing squeeze where you have no card of entry in either ruffing menace. The entry is found in the trump suit and requires a special trump position.

THE OVERTAKING TRUMP SQUEEZE

If all your trumps were winners in the next diagram you would simply cross-ruff to take four tricks. That does not work because East can over-ruff in hearts, so you have to resort to the overtaking trump squeeze.

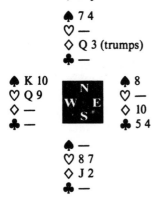

```
            ♠ 7 4
            ♡ —
            ◇ Q 3 (trumps)
            ♣ —
  ♠ K 10              ♠ 8
  ♡ Q 9               ♡ —
  ◇ —                 ◇ 10
  ♣ —                 ♣ 5 4
            ♠ —
            ♡ 8 7
            ◇ J 2
            ♣ —
```

The jack of diamonds is played from hand and West cannot cope. If he throws a heart, you play low from dummy and ruff a heart to establish an extra trick.

If West parts with a spade, you overtake the jack of diamonds with the queen and ruff out the spade stopper.

In this squeeze there has to be a trump of winning rank in both hands, the higher-ranking of these lying over the defender to be squeezed.

Here is an example from practical play.

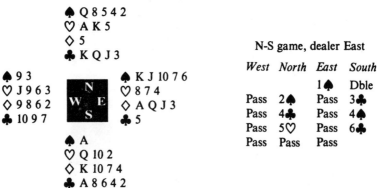

```
            ♠ Q 8 5 4 2
            ♡ A K 5
            ◇ 5
            ♣ K Q J 3
  ♠ 9 3               ♠ K J 10 7 6
  ♡ J 9 6 3           ♡ 8 7 4
  ◇ 9 8 6 2           ◇ A Q J 3
  ♣ 10 9 7            ♣ 5
            ♠ A
            ♡ Q 10 2
            ◇ K 10 7 4
            ♣ A 8 6 4 2
```

N-S game, dealer East

West	North	East	South
		1♠	Dble
Pass	2♠	Pass	3♣
Pass	4♣	Pass	4♠
Pass	5♡	Pass	6♣
Pass	Pass	Pass	

West leads the nine of spades to your ace. You enter dummy with the jack of clubs and play the singleton diamond. East goes up with the ace and returns the eight of hearts to dummy's king. When you play the queen of clubs East discards a heart. How should you continue?

[66]

If the trumps had been 2–2 you would have made your contract easily on a cross-ruff. This is no longer possible, for West is sure to over-ruff if you attempt to ruff spades in your hand. But it should be possible to ruff one spade with impunity, for if East had held six spades he would surely have played a spade when in with the ace of diamonds. Also, East should have the outstanding diamond honours for his opening bid, in which

case it must be possible to catch him in a positional ruffing squeeze of the overtaking type. Ruff a spade to balance the trump position, cash the king of diamonds, throwing a spade from dummy, play off the queen of hearts and continue with a heart to the ace. Now the stage is set for the squeeze.

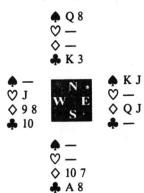

```
            ♠ Q 8
            ♡ —
            ◇ —
            ♣ K 3
♠ —                   ♠ K J
♡ J                   ♡ —
◇ 9 8                 ◇ Q J
♣ 10                  ♣ —
            ♠ —
            ♡ —
            ◇ 10 7
            ♣ A 8
```

When the king of clubs is played East has to surrender. No ambiguity arises since East is known to have started with exactly five spades.

This is our first encounter with a squeeze that uses an entry-shifting mechanism to pose a dilemma for the defence. When the king of clubs is played in the last diagram declarer can choose, according to East's discard, which hand will win the trick. And West's trump is drawn at the same time. This device is of great value and is employed in a number of other squeezes, as we shall see.

In the overtaking trump squeeze it may be necessary to ruff out a side suit and to do some heavy unblocking in order to prepare the required squeeze matrix. Consider this hand.

♠ J 10 7 3
♡ 8 5 4 2
♢ J 9 6 2
♣ A

Game all, dealer West

West	North	East	South
1♣	Pass	1♢	2♡
2♠	3♡	4♢	4♡
Pass	Pass	Pass	

♠ A
♡ A Q J 10 9 7
♢ 8 7
♣ J 8 4 3

West leads the five of diamonds, East winning with the ten when you play low from dummy. East continues with the ace of diamonds, West discarding a club, and then the king of diamonds. You ruff with the queen of hearts, but West over-ruffs with the king and returns a club to dummy's ace. How should you continue?

There will be no difficulty if the remaining trumps fall in one round or if West has them both, for a cross-ruff will then see you home. But you have to envisage the worst possible distribution in such situations. Suppose West began with singletons in both red suits. He will then have five spades and six clubs and the cross-ruff will not work, for East will be in a position to over-ruff on the third round of clubs. This is the distribution you have to guard against.

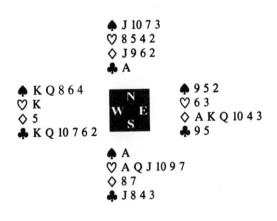

♠ J 10 7 3
♡ 8 5 4 2
♢ J 9 6 2
♣ A

♠ K Q 8 6 4
♡ K
♢ 5
♣ K Q 10 7 6 2

♠ 9 5 2
♡ 6 3
♢ A K Q 10 4 3
♣ 9 5

♠ A
♡ A Q J 10 9 7
♢ 8 7
♣ J 8 4 3

Because of the lamentable disconnection in the black suits, your only hope is an overtaking trump squeeze against West and you know that you need a balanced trump matrix to bring this off. Play the jack of diamonds at trick five and ruff with the ace of hearts. Continue with the jack of hearts to test the trumps. When West shows out you know the position must be as shown in the diagram.

Now cash the ace of spades and play the seven of hearts to apply pressure. West finds himself with no good discard. If he parts with a spade, you overtake with the eight of hearts and ruff out the spades.

If West chooses to discard a club, you stay in hand with the seven of hearts and set up your tenth trick in clubs.

```
                 ♠ J 10 7 3
                 ♡ 8 5 4
                 ◇ —
                 ♣ —
  ♠ K Q 8 6      N        ♠ 9 5 2
  ♡ —                     ♡ 6
  ◇ —         W      E    ◇ 4 3
  ♣ K Q 10       S        ♣ 5
                 ♠ A
                 ♡ 10 9 7
                 ◇ —
                 ♣ J 8 4
```

6

Squeeze Defence

One bonus arising from the study of squeeze play is that you acquire a new perspective in defence. While continuing to apply normal defensive techniques at the table, you also start to take account of the squeeze potential.

It is more difficult to recognise a squeeze position from a defender's seat, but as with all bridge skills this is something that comes with practice. Accurate card-reading is the key. You have to keep a close watch on declarer's actual and potential tricks. When it appears that straightforward play will leave declarer a trick short of his contract, it is time to take a hard look at the squeeze possibilities.

We have already noted points of defensive interest in some of the earlier hands. Now we have to introduce order to the subject by examining the defensive options one by one. There are several distinct lines along which a successful defence may be directed. The three features essential to the declarer for the execution of any squeeze are: entries, menaces and timing. All three are vulnerable to a pre-emptive strike which can render the squeeze still-born. At the outset it must be emphasised that opportunities for blighting the development of a squeeze usually occur at an early stage while you still retain the lead. If chances are missed at this point there may be no recovery. There is little you can do once you are in the grip of an established squeeze.

THE ATTACK ON ENTRIES

No squeeze can function unless the entry position is satisfactory and there are many opportunities for the defenders to take out a vital entry. Consider this hand.

♠ 10 8 7 3
♡ A K 7
◇ J
♣ Q 10 8 5 4

Game all, dealer South

♠ K Q J 4
♡ 10 5
◇ Q 10 6 4 3
♣ 9 2

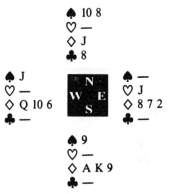

♠ 6 2
♡ J 9 8 6 3
◇ 8 7 2
♣ 7 6 3

♠ A 9 5
♡ Q 4 2
◇ A K 9 5
♣ A K J

South	West	North	East
2NT	Pass	3♣	Pass
3◇	Pass	3♠	Pass
3NT	Pass	4NT	Pass
6NT	Pass	Pass	Pass

West leads the king of spades which holds the first trick. If he continues unimaginatively with the queen of spades, South will make his contract. After winning the spade ace he will run three hearts and five clubs, the last of which will inflict an automatic spade-diamond squeeze on West in the diagram position.

♠ 10 8
♡ —
◇ J
♣ 8

♠ J
♡ —
◇ Q 10 6
♣ —

♠ —
♡ J
◇ 8 7 2
♣ —

♠ 9
♡ —
◇ A K 9
♣ —

When the last club is played, South discards his spade and West has to surrender.

It requires no enormous effort on West's part to foresee this squeeze. He cannot really imagine that South is missing the ace of spades. Declarer's tricks can be counted as five clubs, no more than three hearts (since he did not bid the suit), two diamonds and one spade, making eleven altogether. Only a squeeze in spades and diamonds might provide a twelfth trick. West can see that dummy has no entry in either menace suit, which means that the squeeze card would have to be in dummy. The squeeze would, in fact, be the automatic type, with the short spade menace in dummy and the long diamond menace in declarer's hand.

Having reached this point in his deliberations, West has only a short step to take to find the killing switch to the queen of diamonds at trick two. This defeats the squeeze by removing the entry to the long menace.

LOOKING AFTER PARTNER

The defence can be difficult when you have to think of partner's problems as well as your own. Taking the proper measures to protect partner from a developing squeeze may call for a great deal of foresight on your part.

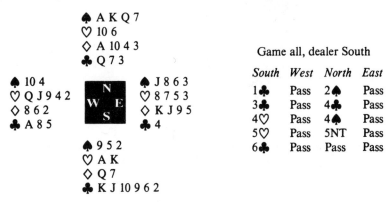

♠ A K Q 7
♡ 10 6
◇ A 10 4 3
♣ Q 7 3

♠ 10 4
♡ Q J 9 4 2
◇ 8 6 2
♣ A 8 5

♠ J 8 6 3
♡ 8 7 5 3
◇ K J 9 5
♣ 4

♠ 9 5 2
♡ A K
◇ Q 7
♣ K J 10 9 6 2

Game all, dealer South

South	West	North	East
1♣	Pass	2♠	Pass
3♣	Pass	4♣	Pass
4♡	Pass	4♠	Pass
5♡	Pass	5NT	Pass
6♣	Pass	Pass	Pass

West leads the queen of hearts against the slam, East playing the five and South the ace. A trump is played to dummy's queen and a second trump is returned.

East is likely to discard the nine of diamonds on this trick, and West may be tempted to win and switch to a diamond. This would be quite the wrong defence, however. The initial lead of a diamond would have broken the contract, but now it is too late. On a diamond switch,

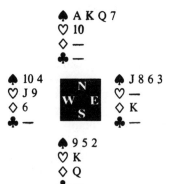

♠ A K Q 7
♡ 10
◇ —
♣ —

♠ 10 4
♡ J 9
◇ 6
♣ —

♠ J 8 6 3
♡ —
◇ K
♣ —

♠ 9 5 2
♡ K
◇ Q
♣ —

declarer would win with the ace and play off all his trumps to reach the diagram position.

The play of the king of hearts now squeezes East automatically in diamonds and spades and the slam rolls home.

West should be able to work this out in advance. He can count declarer's tricks as five trumps, three spades, two hearts and a diamond— a total of eleven. If the contract is to be defeated, East needs to hold the king of diamonds and a spade stopper, but the danger of a squeeze against partner is clear. The correct defence is to hold up the club ace until the third round and then cut communications with a further heart lead. This makes it impossible for declarer to employ the Vienna Coup in diamonds, for if he plays off the ace he has no way back to hand to run the clubs. With the diamond suit blocked, dummy is squeezed before East and the slam has to go one down.

It is surprising how often it is necessary to defend in a roundabout way—shunning the suit where your tricks have to come from and attacking entries elsewhere.

```
              ♠ A K Q 2
              ♡ A 10
              ◇ 7 2
              ♣ J 9 4 3 2
♠ 9 7 3                        ♠ J 10 8 4
♡ 6 5              N            ♡ 8 4 3 2
◇ A K Q 10 9 8 3  W   E         ◇ J 5
♣ K                  S          ♣ Q 10 6
              ♠ 6 5
              ♡ K Q J 9 7
Game all,     ◇ 6 4
dealer North  ♣ A 8 7 5
```

West	North	East	South
	1♣	Pass	1♡
3◇	Pass	Pass	4♣
Pass	4♡	Pass	Pass
Pass			

Everyone follows to two rounds of diamonds. What do you do now?

Declarer is not likely to have more than five trumps on this auction and partner could conceivably have a trump trick. That will be enough to defeat the contract if you are allowed to make your king of clubs.

It is rather more likely that declarer's trumps are solid, in which case you will need two defensive tricks in the club suit. But this does not mean that you should switch to the king of clubs at trick three. Declarer is marked with the ace of clubs, and he might be able to set up a black-suit squeeze against East by allowing your king of clubs to win.

[73]

If declarer has five solid trumps and three spades he is bound to make the contract. But if he has only two spades you can cut communications and break up any squeeze by leading spades twice—at trick three, and again when a club is ducked to your king.

A passive trump switch at trick three will not be good enough. Declarer will draw trumps in four rounds, discarding clubs from dummy, and then concede a club to your king. You may attack the spades now, but it is too late. South wins and plays a club to his ace in this position:

The play of the nine of hearts spells ruination for East, whether he discards a spade or a club.

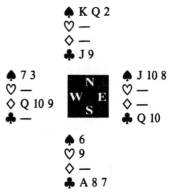

```
          ♠ K Q 2
          ♡ —
          ♢ —
          ♣ J 9
♠ 7 3                    ♠ J 10 8
♡ —         N           ♡ —
♢ Q 10 9  W   E         ♢ —
♣ —         S           ♣ Q 10
          ♠ 6
          ♡ 9
          ♢ —
          ♣ A 8 7
```

DEFEATING A CRISS-CROSS

In the criss-cross squeeze, you will remember, declarer has a blocked entry position in each of the vital suits. Attacking the entries in one suit or the other can cause the squeeze to evaporate. Here is an example.

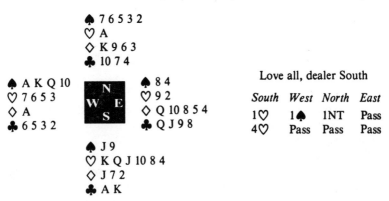

```
          ♠ 7 6 5 3 2
          ♡ A
          ♢ K 9 6 3
          ♣ 10 7 4
♠ A K Q 10              ♠ 8 4
♡ 7 6 5 3     N        ♡ 9 2
♢ A        W   E       ♢ Q 10 8 5 4
♣ 6 5 3 2     S        ♣ Q J 9 8
          ♠ J 9
          ♡ K Q J 10 8 4
          ♢ J 7 2
          ♣ A K
```

Love all, dealer South

South	West	North	East
1♡	1♠	1NT	Pass
4♡	Pass	Pass	Pass

You start, naturally enough, with the ace and king of spades. How should you continue?

If your trumps were a little stronger you might try a third round of spades, hoping that partner could produce an uppercut. But South is marked with six trumps and there can be no real chance of promoting a trump for the defence. A spade continuation would simply allow declarer to set up a long spade on the table.

There is also little point in cashing the ace of diamonds and trying to put partner in to give you a ruff. To account for his strong bidding South must surely have the ace of clubs and probably the king as well. Six trumps, two clubs and a diamond add up to nine tricks. The queen of diamonds would give declarer a tenth trick, but partner could have that card along with some goodies in clubs. The danger is that there might be a minor-suit squeeze against East. If declarer has three clubs and two diamonds there can be no effective defence, but if he has the ace and king of clubs (or ace and queen) doubleton you can break up his criss-cross squeeze by playing a club at trick three and another club when you are in with the ace of diamonds. You cannot tell if this defence will work, but there is nothing else worth trying.

If you switch to a trump at trick three, or if you cash the ace of diamonds before playing a club, declarer has no difficulty in arriving at the position shown in the diagram.

The nine of diamonds is discarded from dummy when the last heart is played and East may as well tear up his cards.

The situation is quite different if the club winners are prematurely removed from the declarer's hand. All that is left is a positional squeeze, which fails because dummy has to discard ahead of East.

```
              ♠ —
              ♡ —
              ◇ K 9
              ♣ 10 7
   ♠ Q        N        ♠ —
   ♡ —     W     E     ♡ —
   ◇ —        S        ◇ Q 10
   ♣ 5 3 2             ♣ Q J
              ♠ —
              ♡ 8
              ◇ J 7
              ♣ K
```

AVERTING A RUFFING SQUEEZE

On the last hand a repeated attack on one of the key suits was required. This is not always the case. In the ruffing squeeze, where declarer needs to preserve two entries in the hand containing the ruffing menace, a single thrust may be enough to kill the squeeze.

```
              ♠ J 7 6 3
              ♡ A K 4 2
              ◇ A 9 4
              ♣ Q 3
♠ 9 5                            ♠ A K Q 10 8 4
♡ 9 8 6                         ♡ Q J 3
◇ 10 7 2                        ◇ 5
♣ J 10 7 5 4                    ♣ 9 8 6
              ♠ 2
              ♡ 10 7 5
Game all,     ◇ K Q J 8 6 3
dealer North  ♣ A K 2
```

West	North	East	South
	1NT	2♠	4◇
Pass	4♡	Pass	4NT
Pass	5♡	Pass	6◇
Pass	Pass	Pass	

Take the East seat for this hand and see if you can find a way of defeating six diamonds. West leads the nine of spades, the jack is played from dummy and you win with the queen. What now?

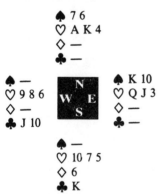

```
              ♠ 7 6
              ♡ A K 4
              ◇ —
              ♣ —
♠ —                    ♠ K 10
♡ 9 8 6                ♡ Q J 3
◇ —                    ◇ —
♣ J 10                 ♣ —
              ♠ —
              ♡ 10 7 5
              ◇ 6
              ♣ K
```

You surely don't expect to be able to cash a second spade. A spade continuation would, in fact, be highly dangerous. South would ruff, play four rounds of trumps and then three rounds of clubs to catch you in a major-suit ruffing squeeze.

On the play of the king of clubs the four of hearts would be discarded from dummy and you would have no good discard. Whether you parted with a spade or a heart, South would make the rest of the tricks.

Naturally you cannot be sure that South has the ten of hearts as a menace for his ruffing squeeze, but you should always assume the worst in such situations. A switch to the queen of hearts at trick two can do no harm, and in this case it does a great deal of good. By removing a vital entry it kills the ruffing squeeze stone dead.

Sometimes in trying to avoid one squeeze a defender falls prey to another. The next deal, which comes from an American National Championship of some years ago, shows the close relationship that exists between the criss-cross and the ruffing squeeze.

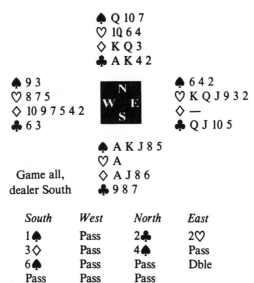

```
                    ♠ Q 10 7
                    ♡ 10 6 4
                    ◇ K Q 3
                    ♣ A K 4 2
   ♠ 9 3                            ♠ 6 4 2
   ♡ 8 7 5              N           ♡ K Q J 9 3 2
   ◇ 10 9 7 5 4 2    W     E        ◇ —
   ♣ 6 3                S           ♣ Q J 10 5
                    ♠ A K J 8 5
                    ♡ A
   Game all,         ◇ A J 8 6
   dealer South      ♣ 9 8 7
```

South	West	North	East
1♠	Pass	2♣	2♡
3◇	Pass	4♠	Pass
6♠	Pass	Pass	Dble
Pass	Pass	Pass	

It seems quite reasonable for East to make a Lightner double of six spades, hoping to score a diamond ruff and another trick in the wash. The diamond ruff duly materialised but the other trick did not.

After ruffing the initial diamond lead East switched to the king of hearts to knock out the ace. Declarer drew trumps, played off his diamonds and reverted to trumps. This was the position with five tricks to go:

The four of clubs was discarded from dummy on the jack of spades, and the ruffing squeeze had East firmly in its toils.

It was suggested that East should have seen the danger looming ahead

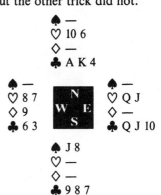

```
         ♠ —
         ♡ 10 6
         ◇ —
         ♣ A K 4
   ♠ —              ♠ —
   ♡ 8 7     N      ♡ Q J
   ◇ 9    W     E   ◇ —
   ♣ 6 3     S      ♣ Q J 10
         ♠ J 8
         ♡ —
         ◇ —
         ♣ 9 8 7
```

and might have taken counter-measures. If, instead of playing the king of hearts at trick two, he had returned the queen of clubs this would have removed a vital entry from dummy and the ruffing squeeze would have failed.

All this is perfectly true, but a club return would have left East no better off since a new danger rears its head. Winning the club switch, declarer would have run all his trumps and his diamonds to reach the position shown in this diagram.

On the play of the jack of diamonds the four of clubs is thrown from the table and again East is caught—this time in a criss-cross squeeze.

Sometimes a defender just can't win.

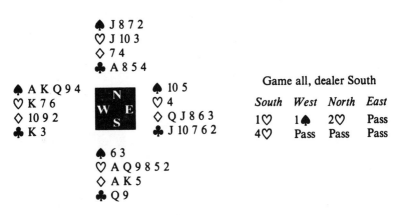

THE ATTACK ON MENACES

When it is not possible for one reason or another to launch an assault on the entries needed for the squeeze, the defence has to be tackled in a different way. Sometimes it will be possible to wipe out one of declarer's menaces by means of a sustained attack on the menace suit.

♠ J 8 7 2
♡ J 10 3
◊ 7 4
♣ A 8 5 4

♠ A K Q 9 4   ♠ 10 5
♡ K 7 6   ♡ 4
◊ 10 9 2   ◊ Q J 8 6 3
♣ K 3   ♣ J 10 7 6 2

♠ 6 3
♡ A Q 9 8 5 2
◊ A K 5
♣ Q 9

Game all, dealer South

South	West	North	East
1♡	1♠	2♡	Pass
4♡	Pass	Pass	Pass

This is one of the hands from Chapter Two. West cashed the king and queen of spades and then switched to the ten of diamonds. South ruffed the third round of diamonds with the jack of hearts and ran the heart ten to West's king. West returned a trump, but on the run of the trumps he was caught in a positional squeeze in the black suits.

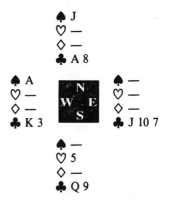

In the diagram position the play of the five of hearts placed West in the familiar dilemma and the contract was made.

West should have seen this squeeze coming from the start and should have taken action to prevent it maturing. An attack on entries is not possible in this case, since West cannot lead a club without giving declarer his tenth trick.

The attack should have been directed against the spade menace with a view to wiping it out completely. After winning the second spade West should continue with a third spade—a small one, since it is essential to make use of partner's trump while he still possesses it. South over-ruffs on the third round of spades, ruffs his third diamond in dummy as before, and runs the ten of hearts to the king. But now West is in a position to destroy the spade menace by continuing with the spade ace. Denied any chance of a squeeze, South has to lose a club trick at the end.

Here is a similar case.

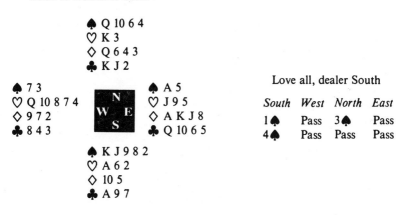

Love all, dealer South

South	West	North	East
1♠	Pass	3♠	Pass
4♠	Pass	Pass	Pass

West leads the seven of diamonds against South's contract of four spades. When dummy plays low you win with the jack and cash the ace,

South playing the ten and West the nine on the second round. How should you continue?

Declarer is marked with the missing aces and he can hardly have a second loser in trumps. Since there is no further diamond to cash it looks as though the setting trick will have to come from clubs. You have to base your defence on the assumption that declarer has a 5-3-2-3 shape along with the nine of clubs. Then, if you fail to take precautions, you may find yourself caught in a minor-suit squeeze.

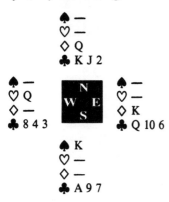

♠ —
♡ —
◇ Q
♣ K J 2

♠ —
♡ Q
◇ —
♣ 8 4 3

♠ —
♡ —
◇ K
♣ Q 10 6

♠ K
♡ —
◇ —
♣ A 9 7

The end position will be as shown in the diagram.

A club is discarded from dummy on the last spade and the inverted automatic squeeze brings you to your knees.

The ending was perfectly foreseeable and the squeeze should not have been allowed to mature. A sustained attack on the diamond menace is the proper medicine. Continue with the king of diamonds at trick three, temporarily establishing a diamond trick for declarer. This does him no good, for you shoot up with the ace on the first round of trumps and continue with the fourth diamond while partner still has a trump. The diamond menace is thus erased and declarer is left with no chance of a squeeze.

DISRUPTING THE TIMING

A third way of preventing a squeeze from maturing is by refusing to allow the declarer to achieve the proper timing. This is mainly an extension of hold-up technique.

As you know, in the basic squeezes declarer often needs to rectify the count by conceding tricks to the defenders at an early stage. Declarer must be in a position to win all the remaining tricks but one before his squeeze will function. There is no reason why the defenders should help him by taking their winners at the first opportunity. By refusing to take your aces and kings at a time convenient to declarer you may make it impossible for him to set up the squeeze matrix that he needs.

Here is a typical case.

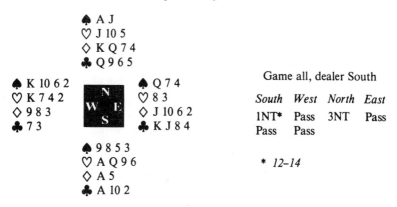

♠ A J
♡ J 10 5
◇ K Q 7 4
♣ Q 9 6 5

♠ K 10 6 2   ♠ Q 7 4
♡ K 7 4 2   ♡ 8 3
◇ 9 8 3   ◇ J 10 6 2
♣ 7 3   ♣ K J 8 4

♠ 9 8 5 3
♡ A Q 9 6
◇ A 5
♣ A 10 2

Game all, dealer South

South	West	North	East
1NT*	Pass	3NT	Pass
Pass	Pass		

* *12–14*

On your lead of the two of spades the jack is played from dummy. East wins with the queen and returns the seven of spades to the ace. The declarer now runs the jack of hearts to your king.

The critical point of the hand has been reached. You are in a position to cash two winning spades, but if you do so the contract will be made. South will throw clubs from dummy on the spades, and after winning your club switch he will run the hearts, squeezing East in the position shown in the diagram.

The queen of clubs is thrown from dummy on the last heart and East has no good discard.

Do you understand what happened? By cashing your spade winners you rectified the count for declarer and tightened up the squeeze position against partner. This was quite unnecessary.

The bidding had marked partner with something good in the minor suits. If he has an ace it does not

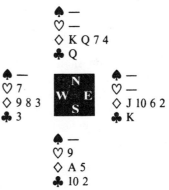

♠ —
♡ —
◇ K Q 7 4
♣ Q

♠ —   ♠ —
♡ 7   ♡ —
◇ 9 8 3   ◇ J 10 6 2
♣ 3   ♣ K

♠ —
♡ 9
◇ A 5
♣ 10 2

matter how you defend. But in the actual case, where he has king and jack in clubs plus a diamond stopper, it is essential to switch to a club after winning the king of hearts. This sets up a fifth trick for the defence and destroys all possibility of a squeeze.

Now try defending a slam from the East seat.

♠ A 7 4
♡ K Q 8 3
◇ Q 10
♣ A 7 6 2

Love all, dealer South

South	West	North	East
1◇	Pass	1♡	Pass
1NT*	Pass	4NT	Pass
6NT	Pass	Pass	Pass

♠ Q J 10 6 2   ♠ 9 5
♡ 10 6   ♡ A J 9 5 2
◇ 4 2   ◇ 9 8 6 3
♣ J 9 5 4   ♣ 8 3

♠ K 8 3
♡ 7 4
◇ A K J 7 5
♣ K Q 10

* *15–16*

West leads the queen of spades to declarer's king. At trick two South plays a heart on which West plays the ten and dummy the queen.

The fate of the contract depends on how you play to this trick. If you win, that will be the end of the defence. No matter what you return, South will cash the king and queen of clubs, the king of hearts, the ace of spades and five rounds of diamonds, inflicting an automatic black-suit squeeze on West.

The play of the last diamond puts West through the mangle and the slam is made.

Naturally you should not allow this to happen. You prevent it by refusing to take the ace of hearts at trick two. This is not a double-dummy exercise but a play based on logic. A defender with any knowledge of squeeze play should be able to see the danger looming ahead. Declarer is known to have only three winners in the major suits, so he needs nine

♠ 7
♡ —
◇ —
♣ A 7

♠ J   ♠ —
♡ —   ♡ J 9 5
◇ —   ◇ —
♣ J 9   ♣ —

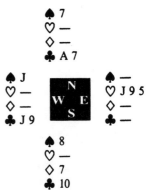

♠ 8
♡ —
◇ 7
♣ 10

tricks from the minors to make his slam. In practice five diamond winners and three club winners will be enough, for there is bound to be a black-suit squeeze against West if declarer is permitted to rectify his loser count. The hold-up in hearts stands out a mile.

If you play low smoothly enough there is a good chance that declarer, placing West with the ace, will return to hand and play a second heart to the king. That will be three down! At any rate the duck will defeat the contract. With the count unrectified, South is unable to bring pressure to bear.

There are many situations where it is dangerous to cash a trick. Look at what happened on the next hand.

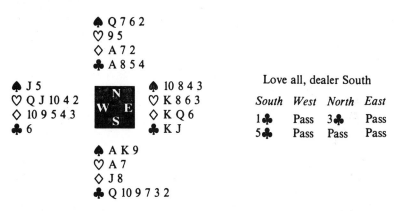

```
                ♠ Q 7 6 2
                ♡ 9 5
                ◇ A 7 2
                ♣ A 8 5 4
♠ J 5                           ♠ 10 8 4 3
♡ Q J 10 4 2      N             ♡ K 8 6 3
◇ 10 9 5 4 3   W     E          ◇ K Q 6
♣ 6               S             ♣ K J
                ♠ A K 9
                ♡ A 7
                ◇ J 8
                ♣ Q 10 9 7 3 2
```

Love all, dealer South

South	West	North	East
1♣	Pass	3♣	Pass
5♣	Pass	Pass	Pass

West led the queen of hearts and the ace won the trick. The declarer played a club to the ace and returned a club to East's king, West discarding the three of diamonds. After cashing the king of hearts East switched to the king of diamonds, but this defence was not good enough. Winning the ace of diamonds, South played out his entire club suit, discarding diamonds from the table.

On the play of the last club East was in trouble. He chose to part with a spade, and the declarer made four spade tricks for his contract.

A more alert defender in the East seat might have realised that by cashing the king of hearts he would tighten up a squeeze position against himself. Declarer's tricks can be counted as five clubs, probably three spades and the two red aces—a total

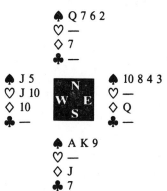

```
        ♠ Q 7 6 2
        ♡ —
        ◇ 7
        ♣ —
♠ J 5              ♠ 10 8 4 3
♡ J 10      N      ♡ —
◇ 10     W     E   ◇ Q
♣ —         S      ♣ —
        ♠ A K 9
        ♡ —
        ◇ J
        ♣ 7
```

of ten. The eleventh might come from a squeeze if East is helpful enough to rectify the count. After winning the king of clubs East should switch immediately to the king of diamonds without cashing the heart winner. The timing is then subtly different and the squeeze fails.

The position is shown in the new diagram. Everyone discards a heart on the last club, and at the end East scores a diamond and a spade instead of his heart trick.

Defence should never be allowed to become a static business. Flexibility is essential, for the defensive plan often has to change to take account of the line of play adopted by the declarer.

The next hand illustrates the point.

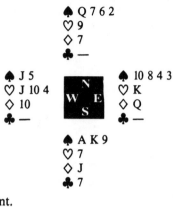

```
        ♠ Q 7 6 2
        ♡ 9
        ◇ 7
        ♣ —
♠ J 5              ♠ 10 8 4 3
♡ J 10 4          ♡ K
◇ 10              ◇ Q
♣ —                ♣ —
        ♠ A K 9
        ♡ 7
        ◇ J
        ♣ 7
```

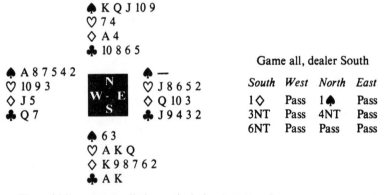

```
        ♠ K Q J 10 9
        ♡ 7 4
        ◇ A 4
        ♣ 10 8 6 5
♠ A 8 7 5 4 2          ♠ —
♡ 10 9 3              ♡ J 8 6 5 2
◇ J 5                ◇ Q 10 3
♣ Q 7                ♣ J 9 4 3 2
        ♠ 6 3
        ♡ A K Q
        ◇ K 9 8 7 6 2
        ♣ A K
```

Game all, dealer South

South	West	North	East
1◇	Pass	1♠	Pass
3NT	Pass	4NT	Pass
6NT	Pass	Pass	Pass

The bidding was a little optimistic, but the final contract is not unreasonable since the declarer can count eleven tricks once the ace of spades has been knocked out. South wins your initial heart lead and plays a spade on which you play low. Dummy's nine wins and East discards a heart.

Declarer is likely to continue with a second spade from dummy, and East will no doubt throw a club this time. You cannot afford to hold off again, for that would enable South to abandon spades and concede the third round of diamonds to East, making his slam with two spade tricks, three hearts, five diamonds and two clubs. Suppose you win the ace of spades and continue with a second heart. Declarer will win, cash his third heart and the top clubs (the Vienna Coup), then play a diamond to the ace and run the spades. On the play of the last spade East will be hopelessly squeezed in the diagram position.

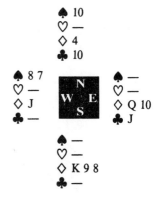

Whether East discards a club or a diamond on the last spade declarer takes the rest of the tricks.

Naturally you saw this trouble looming ahead and took appropriate counter-measures by switching to a diamond after winning the ace of spades. This takes out dummy's only remaining entry before declarer is ready to use it, and the squeeze founders because the club and heart winners have not been played off.

But South could have put you to a different sort of test. Seeing the havoc that a diamond switch would cause, he might have cashed his heart and club winners before playing the second spade. Now a more subtle defence is needed. It will not do to win the second spade and attack the diamond entry, since declarer has already executed his Vienna Coup, aligning the menaces properly for the squeeze. Fortunately declarer can no longer afford to concede a diamond to East, who has established winners to cash. There is therefore no need to take the spade ace on the second round.

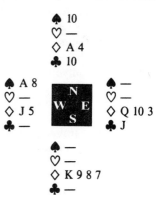

An attack on the timing is now the indicated defence. You have already held up the ace of spades once, and it is just a matter of holding up three more times until the diagram position is reached.

Having failed to lose one of the first nine tricks, South finds that he has to lose two of the last four.

NO SUICIDE

It is vital to find a way of adjusting the timing in your favour when you detect a risk of being subjected to a suicide squeeze.

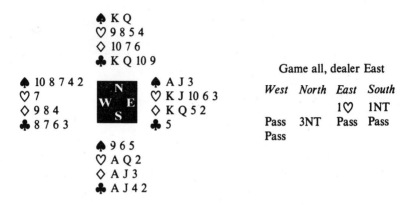

♠ K Q
♡ 9 8 5 4
◇ 10 7 6
♣ K Q 10 9

♠ 10 8 7 4 2
♡ 7
◇ 9 8 4
♣ 8 7 6 3

♠ A J 3
♡ K J 10 6 3
◇ K Q 5 2
♣ 5

♠ 9 6 5
♡ A Q 2
◇ A J 3
♣ A J 4 2

Game all, dealer East

West	North	East	South
		1♡	1NT
Pass	3NT	Pass	Pass
Pass			

Ignoring your opening bid, West leads the four of spades against three no trumps. How do you plan the defence?

Just about the only honour card West can possess is the ten of spades, but that may be enough to defeat the contract if he has a five-card suit, as is likely from his lead. It seems obvious to capture the queen of spades with the ace and return the jack to dummy's king, but there is a hidden danger in this course. South is known to have a third spade, and he may well cross to his hand with a club and play it, thereby cutting the link between you and your partner and assuring himself of a ninth trick. If partner runs all his spades, the position will be as shown in the diagram.

No matter what West now plays, three rounds of clubs will make mincemeat of your hand.

It does not help the defence if West refuses to cash all his spades. After any switch South can establish his ninth trick in diamonds

The only way to avoid hara-kiri on this hand is to play the jack of spades under dummy's queen at

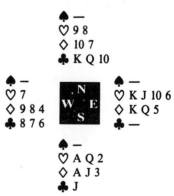

♠ —
♡ 9 8
◇ 10 7
♣ K Q 10

♠ —
♡ 7
◇ 9 8 4
♣ 8 7 6

♠ —
♡ K J 10 6
◇ K Q 5
♣ —

♠ —
♡ A Q 2
◇ A J 3
♣ J

trick one. Now the timing is in your favour. If South continues with the king of spades to your ace, you can switch to the king of diamonds. This establishes a fifth trick for the defence before the spades are run, and declarer has no way of coming to a ninth trick.

A MIGHTY FIVE

One further way of defeating a squeeze is by retaining a card that relieves partner of the burden of protecting a particular suit. The problem is that the card may not always *look* like a potential stopper.

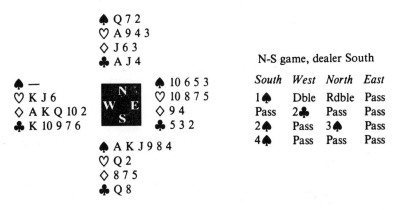

♠ Q 7 2
♡ A 9 4 3
♢ J 6 3
♣ A J 4

N-S game, dealer South

♠ —
♡ K J 6
♢ A K Q 10 2
♣ K 10 9 7 6

♠ 10 6 5 3
♡ 10 8 7 5
♢ 9 4
♣ 5 3 2

♠ A K J 9 8 4
♡ Q 2
♢ 8 7 5
♣ Q 8

South	West	North	East
1♠	Dble	Rdble	Pass
Pass	2♣	Pass	Pass
2♠	Pass	3♠	Pass
4♠	Pass	Pass	Pass

West starts with three top diamonds against South's contract of four spades, and East has to be wide awake to defeat the game.

For a start he must ruff the third diamond. Otherwise West will be endplayed and forced to concede the tenth trick whether he switches or continues with a fourth diamond. Perhaps West should have led the ten of diamonds on the third round, but he was afraid that East might have to ruff with a natural trump trick.

Having surmounted the first hurdle by ruffing the third diamond, East will no doubt return a heart. South will play low and the jack will force out dummy's ace. Next will come six rounds of trumps and East must be careful not to part with a club. His hearts are worthless, but the lowly five of clubs is big enough to contain the threat of dummy's four. The end position is shown in the diagram.

When the last spade is played West discards a club, relying on his partner for protection in this suit. Sure enough, East's cards are just good enough.

At trick four East may choose to return a club instead of a heart. That will be all right as long as he doesn't lead the mighty five.

```
              ♠ —
              ♡ 9
              ◇ —
              ♣ A J 4
♠ —                      ♠ —
♡ K          N           ♡ 10
◇ —       W     E        ◇ —
♣ K 10 9     S           ♣ 5 3 2
              ♠ 8
              ♡ Q
              ◇ —
              ♣ Q 8
```

DECEPTIVE DISCARDING

When you are in the grip of a fully-established squeeze there is not a great deal you can do about it. Those squeezes where declarer has to retain top cards in more than one suit, or more than one top card in a vital suit, like the criss-cross and the ruffing squeeze, usually contain an element of ambiguity, however. Declarer can always prevail if he reads the position correctly. But you may be able to point him in the wrong direction by means of deceptive discarding.

Here is an example.

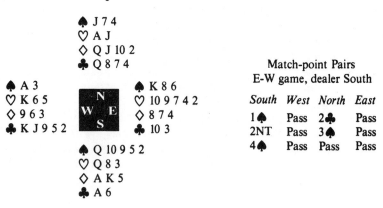

```
              ♠ J 7 4
              ♡ A J
              ◇ Q J 10 2
              ♣ Q 8 7 4
♠ A 3                      ♠ K 8 6
♡ K 6 5        N           ♡ 10 9 7 4 2
◇ 9 6 3     W     E        ◇ 8 7 4
♣ K J 9 5 2    S           ♣ 10 3
              ♠ Q 10 9 5 2
              ♡ Q 8 3
              ◇ A K 5
              ♣ A 6
```

Match-point Pairs
E-W game, dealer South

South	West	North	East
1♠	Pass	2♣	Pass
2NT	Pass	3♠	Pass
4♠	Pass	Pass	Pass

The defence gets off to a good start with three rounds of trumps, denying declarer a heart ruff in dummy.

[88]

South is safe for ten tricks, of course, but at pairs he will be keen to scoop in the valuable overtrick. Since West has both missing kings, declarer can in fact make eleven tricks by means of a criss-cross squeeze. He wins the third trump in hand, finesses the jack of hearts, returns to hand with the king of diamonds and plays off the last two trumps.

Having already discarded a club on the third round of spades, West has to do some rapid thinking about his discards. Declarer is marked with the minor-suit aces and West should see the criss-cross coming. In such cases the only defence is to make use of the ambiguity inherent in the position and try, by deceptive discarding, to give declarer a false picture. West might discard his remaining small heart on the fourth spade and a club on the fifth one. South will then run the diamonds, throwing the six of clubs from his hand. West should discard the club jack on this trick, concealing the nine. There is now a good chance that South will go astray by cashing the ace of clubs next.

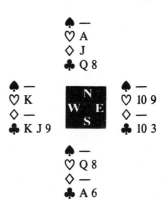

```
                ♠ —
                ♡ A
                ◇ J
                ♣ Q 8
♠ —                        ♠ —
♡ K          N             ♡ 10 9
◇ —      W       E         ◇ —
♣ K J 9      S             ♣ 10 3
                ♠ —
                ♡ Q 8
                ◇ —
                ♣ A 6
```

7

Exercises

This section is included to give readers the opportunity to put their knowledge of squeeze play and defence to practical use. Only two hands are shown to begin with so that you have to work under conditions that approximate to real life. It is by working through a large body of problems of this sort that a player can gain the confidence to deal with similar situations at the bridge table.

You will meet with nothing in the exercises that has not been covered in the earlier chapters, so your performance in this test will give a good indication of how much you have absorbed from a first reading of the book. Make a real effort to solve each problem by yourself before going on to read the solution. Award yourself five points for each correct answer, and your score at the end of the twenty problems will give you a percentage figure. Anything over 60% is highly satisfactory for anyone new to squeeze play. If your score is less than 60%, perhaps you should read the book once more and try the exercises again in a month or two.

Exercises

Exercise 1

♠ 7 5 4 2
♡ 7 4
◇ A K 6
♣ K Q 7 2

♠ A K Q
♡ A 3
◇ Q J 10 3
♣ A 6 5 4

Game all, dealer South

South	West	North	East
2NT	Pass	4NT	Pass
6NT	Pass	Pass	Pass

West leads the ten of spades and when dummy goes down you see that six clubs might have been an easier contract. With this particular partner you had no machinery for reaching six clubs.

How do you plan the play in six no trumps?

Exercise 2

♠ A Q J 4
♡ K 5
◇ 9 8 6 3
♣ A K J

♠ 10 2
♡ A Q J 10 8 6
◇ 7 4 2
♣ 8 5

Game all, dealer East

West	North	East	South
		1◇	1♡
Pass	2◇	Pass	2♡
Pass	4♡	Pass	Pass
Pass			

West leads the queen of diamonds and East overtakes with the king. East continues with the ace and jack of diamonds on which West discards two clubs. When East persists with the ten of diamonds you ruff high and West throws a spade. Both defenders follow suit when you play a heart to the king. How should you continue?

[91]

Exercise 3

♠ 10 9 3
♡ Q 9 4 3
◇ K Q J
♣ A 10 6

Game all, dealer East

♠ A 7
♡ J 10 5
◇ 10 9 7 3 2
♣ 8 4 3

```
  N
W   E
  S
```

West	North	East	South
		1♡	1♠
2♡	3♠	Pass	4♠
Pass	Pass	Pass	

You lead the jack of hearts on which dummy plays the three, East the two and South the seven. When you continue with the ten of hearts it is covered by the queen and king. South ruffs and plays a low spade. How do you defend?

Exercise 4

♠ Q 7 5
♡ A 8 6 3
◇ 10 7 5 4
♣ 10 3

Game all, dealer South

```
  N
W   E
  S
```

♠ A K J
♡ K 10 4
◇ J
♣ A K Q J 7 2

South	West	North	East
2♣	Pass	2◇	Pass
3♣	Pass	3♡	Pass
3♠	Pass	5♣	Pass
6♣	Pass	Pass	Pass

West leads the nine of clubs and it is apparent that you have been a little optimistic in the bidding. How do you plan the play?

Exercise 5

♠ J 5 4
♡ J 9 6
◇ A 10 3
♣ K Q 6 3

Love all, dealer North

West	North	East	South
	Pass	Pass	1NT
Pass	3NT	Pass	Pass
Pass			

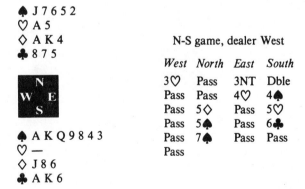

♠ A Q 7
♡ K 5 2
◇ Q J 9 4
♣ A 7 2

West leads the jack of clubs to the three, five and ace. The queen of diamonds wins the second trick, but when you continue with a diamond to the ten East produces the king and switches to the queen of hearts. Ouch! How do you plan the play?

Exercise 6

♠ J 7 6 5 2
♡ A 5
◇ A K 4
♣ 8 7 5

N-S game, dealer West

West	North	East	South
3♡	Pass	3NT	Dble
Pass	Pass	4♡	4♠
Pass	5◇	Pass	5♡
Pass	5♠	Pass	6♣
Pass	7♠	Pass	Pass
Pass			

♠ A K Q 9 8 4 3
♡ —
◇ J 8 6
♣ A K 6

West leads the king of hearts against your grand slam. How do you plan the play?

Exercise 7

♠ 5 2
♡ A 9 8
◇ 10 5 4 2
♣ A K Q 3

N-S game, dealer West

♠ K Q 8 4
♡ J 6 4 2
◇ 9 8
♣ 10 8 7

West	North	East	South
Pass	1NT	2◇*	Dble
3♠	Pass	Pass	5◇
Pass	Pass	Pass	

* *Aspro—spades and a minor*

You start with the king and queen of spades, East playing the three and the jack, South the six and the ten. How should you continue?

Exercise 8

♠ J 9 3
♡ 7 4
◇ J 8 7 2
♣ A Q 6 4

N-S game, dealer South

♠ A Q 10 4
♡ A K Q
◇ A K
♣ K 9 7 3

South	West	North	East
2♣	Pass	2◇	Pass
3NT	Pass	6NT	Pass
Pass	Pass		

West leads the three of diamonds: two, six, king. You cross to the queen of clubs and run the nine of spades, which wins the trick. You continue with the jack of spades, but this time West produces the king and returns the five of diamonds to the seven, four and ace. How should you continue?

Exercise 9

♠ Q 10 4 3
♡ 7 4
◇ K J 3
♣ K Q 8 6

Game all, dealer North

West	North	East	South
	Pass	1♡	1♠
Pass	3♠	Pass	4♠
Pass	Pass	Pass	

♠ A K J 9 5
♡ J 8 5
◇ A 9 4
♣ 5 2

West leads the three of hearts to his partner's king. East continues with the ace and another heart, West playing the queen as you ruff in dummy. After a spade to your ace you play a club from hand. East tops the king with his ace and returns the ten of clubs to dummy's queen. When you cash the queen of spades East follows but West discards a diamond. How should you continue?

Exercise 10

Love all, dealer South

South	West	North	East
1♣	1◇	3NT	Pass
4♣	Pass	4◇	Pass
6♣	Pass	Pass	Pass

♠ Q 7 4
♡ Q 5 4
◇ A Q 10 3
♣ A 8 5

♠ 10 9 6
♡ 9 7 6 2
◇ 7 4 2
♣ K 4 3

West leads the jack of hearts. South wins with the king and runs the queen of clubs. You allow this to hold, and on the next club West discards the eight of spades. The club ace wins and declarer plays a third club to your king, West discarding the five of diamonds. What do you return?

[95]

Exercise 11

♠ A K 9 4
♡ J 5 4
◇ A K 6 5
♣ J 5

Game all, dealer South

South	West	North	East
1♡	Pass	1♠	Pass
2♡	Pass	3◇	Pass
4♣	Pass	5♡	Pass
6♡	Pass	Pass	Pass

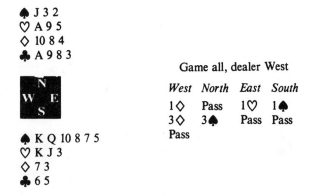

♠ 5 3
♡ A Q 10 6 3 2
◇ 9 4 3
♣ A K

West leads the eight of spades to dummy's ace. How do you plan the play?

Exercise 12

♠ J 3 2
♡ A 9 5
◇ 10 8 4
♣ A 9 8 3

Game all, dealer West

West	North	East	South
1◇	Pass	1♡	1♠
3◇	3♠	Pass	Pass
Pass			

♠ K Q 10 8 7 5
♡ K J 3
◇ 7 3
♣ 6 5

West starts with the ace, king and queen of diamonds, East discarding a heart as you ruff the third round. The king of spades is captured by West's ace, East following suit. West now switches to the jack of clubs. How do you plan the play?

[96]

Exercise 13

♠ 9 8 5 3
♡ K 4
◇ K 9 6 2
♣ 7 6 4

♠ A K J 10 4
♡ 7 6
◇ Q J 8 5
♣ 8 3

N-S game, dealer South

South	West	North	East
2♡*	2♠	4♡	Pass
6♡	Pass	Pass	Pass

* *Acol Two*

You attack with the ace of spades, East playing the two and South the seven. How should you continue?

Exercise 14

♠ J 6 5
♡ J 6 5 2
◇ Q 7 5
♣ A 5 3

♠ A K Q 10 8
♡ A 10
◇ 10 8 4 3
♣ K 7

N-S game, dealer South

South	West	North	East
1♠	Pass	2♠	Pass
4♠	Pass	Pass	Pass

West, who normally leads A from A K x, starts with the king of diamonds. He continues with the ace of diamonds and switches to the jack of clubs. You win in hand with the king, play a spade to dummy's jack and return a heart, putting in the ten when East plays low. West wins with the king and plays a second club to knock out dummy's ace. How do you plan to bring home the game?

Exercise 15

♠ Q J 9 8 3
♡ 10 3
◇ A 10
♣ A K Q 6

N-S game, dealer South

South	West	North	East
1NT	Pass	2♡*	Dble
2♠	Pass	3♣	Pass
4♠	Pass	5◇	Pass
5♡	Pass	6♠	Pass
Pass	Pass		

♠ A K 10
♡ A 7 6 4
◇ Q J 5
♣ 7 4 3

* *Transfer to spades*

West leads the eight of hearts to the three, nine and ace. How do you plan the play?

Exercise 16

♠ J 6 3
♡ A J 5
◇ A Q J 10 4
♣ 8 6

Love all, dealer North

♠ Q 8 5 4
♡ K Q 2
◇ 9 3
♣ A 10 7 2

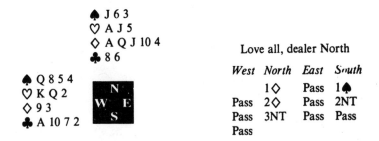

West	North	East	South
	1◇	Pass	1♠
Pass	2◇	Pass	2NT
Pass	3NT	Pass	Pass
Pass			

On your lead of the two of clubs East plays the queen and South the five. East returns the three of clubs to the nine and ten. How should you continue?

Exercise 17

♠ Q 10 6 3
♡ A 10 5
◇ J 6 4 2
♣ 9 3

Game all, dealer East

West	North	East	South
		1♣	Dble
Pass	1♠	2♣	2◇
Pass	4◇	Pass	5◇
Pass	Pass	Pass	

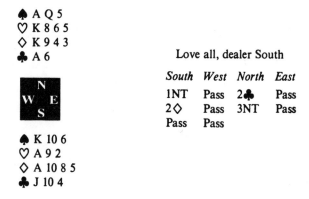

♠ A
♡ K 8 2
◇ A K Q 10 7 5
♣ 8 5 2

The lead of the queen of clubs is overtaken by the king, and East
continues with the ace and then the jack of clubs. West ruffs with the
eight of diamonds on the third round and you over-ruff with dummy's
jack. Both defenders follow suit when you play a diamond to the ace.
How should you continue?

Exercise 18

♠ A Q 5
♡ K 8 6 5
◇ K 9 4 3
♣ A 6

Love all, dealer South

South	West	North	East
1NT	Pass	2♣	Pass
2◇	Pass	3NT	Pass
Pass	Pass		

♠ K 10 6
♡ A 9 2
◇ A 10 8 5
♣ J 10 4

West leads the three of clubs. When you play low from dummy East
wins with the queen and continues with the eight of clubs to the ace,
West playing the two. How do you plan the play?

Exercise 19

♠ J 9 8 5 3 2
♡ J 5
◇ 9 8 3
♣ 4 2

N-S game, dealer East

West	North	East	South
		3♣	3◇*
Pass	4♡	Pass	4NT
Pass	5◇	Pass	5NT
Pass	6♡	Pass	7NT
Pass	Pass	Pass	

* *for takeout*

What do you lead against the grand slam?

Exercise 20

♠ 5
♡ A Q J 9 4
◇ A K
♣ A 10 7 3 2

Game all, dealer East

West	North	East	South
		1♠	Pass
Pass	Dble	2♣	2♡
Pass	3♣	Dble	3♡
Pass	3♠	Dble	4♣
Pass	6♡	Pass	Pass
Pass			

♠ K 8 6 3
♡ K 7 6 3 2
◇ 8 5 4
♣ 5

West leads the eight of clubs to dummy's ace. At trick two you cash the ace of hearts on which East discards the two of diamonds. How should you continue?

[100]

Solution 1

Twelve tricks at no trumps will be easy enough if the clubs break 3–2. If they do not, the only hope is a black-suit squeeze against one defender or the other. At present you have eleven of the thirteen tricks. To bring off a squeeze you need to rectify the loser count by conceding a trick to the opponents. Hearts is the only suit in which you can concede a trick without destroying one of your menaces, and the time to give up the trick is right now. Play a small heart from both hands at trick two.

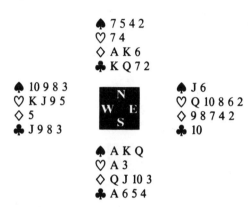

```
              ♠ 7 5 4 2
              ♡ 7 4
              ◇ A K 6
              ♣ K Q 7 2
  ♠ 10 9 8 3              ♠ J 6
  ♡ K J 9 5      N        ♡ Q 10 8 6 2
  ◇ 5        W     E      ◇ 9 8 7 4 2
  ♣ J 9 8 3      S        ♣ 10
              ♠ A K Q
              ♡ A 3
              ◇ Q J 10 3
              ♣ A 6 5 4
```

You can win any return, cash the top spades, the ace of hearts and four diamonds to catch either defender (West, as it happens) in an automatic black-suit squeeze.

It would be a mistake to test any suit before ducking the heart. If you played off the top spades first, West would be able to cash a winning spade when in with the heart. If you played four rounds of diamonds first, East would win the heart and cash a diamond. And if you played two rounds of clubs to test the lie, a club return from West when in with the heart would remove the last club entry and ruin your squeeze.

When you need to rectify the count, do it as early as possible.

Solution 2

You can count nine tricks and the tenth might come from a finesse in either spades or clubs. However, it seems likely that East will have both the king of spades and the queen of clubs for his vulnerable opening bid. So your thoughts should turn in the direction of squeezing East rather than finessing against West. At present both menaces are in dummy and you know that this will not do for a squeeze against East—at least one menace must lie in your own hand. Before playing another round of trumps you must unblock the spades by cashing the ace, a Vienna Coup that establishes the ten of spades as a menace in your hand. Now the run of the trumps will give East more trouble than he can handle.

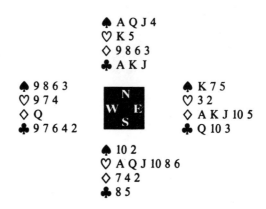

On the long trumps you discard all three remaining spades from the table, and if the spade king does not make an appearance you play for the drop in clubs.

Be sure to note that the squeeze fails if the spade ace is not cashed before a second trump is played.

Solution 3

To defeat this contract you need to find partner with two further tricks. He is not likely to have the king of spades and the ace of diamonds, but he might have one of these cards plus a stopper in clubs. The danger is that partner may eventually be squeezed in hearts and clubs. An attack on clubs is hardly likely to defeat the squeeze, but you should be able to rub out the heart menace by attacking twice more in the suit. You have to take the initiative, for partner cannot attack hearts at the moment without establishing dummy's nine. You should therefore shoot up with the ace of spades and return your heart.

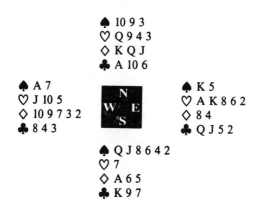

```
              ♠ 10 9 3
              ♡ Q 9 4 3
              ◇ K Q J
              ♣ A 10 6
♠ A 7                        ♠ K 5
♡ J 10 5          N          ♡ A K 8 6 2
◇ 10 9 7 3 2   W   E         ◇ 8 4
♣ 8 4 3          S           ♣ Q J 5 2
              ♠ Q J 8 6 4 2
              ♡ 7
              ◇ A 6 5
              ♣ K 9 7
```

When East comes in with the king of spades he plays a fourth heart, obliterating the menace and removing all danger of a squeeze.

Note that on a spade return or a diamond switch, declarer can organise an inverted automatic squeeze against East, using the split three-card menace in clubs.

On a club return, declarer can win in hand, knock out the king of spades, win the diamond return and play three more trumps followed by dummy's diamonds to produce a ruffing squeeze.

Solution 4

Apart from the remote possibility of finding someone with the Q J doubleton in hearts (or West with a singleton honour), there is a chance of a squeeze if someone has length in both red suits. Some ruffing will be essential to isolate the diamond stopper in the hand of one defender, and you must preserve every available entry in dummy.

Win the trump lead in hand and play the jack of diamonds. This serves the dual purpose of rectifying the loser count and preparing for diamond ruffs. If a heart comes back you must win with the king, then cross to the ten of clubs and ruff a diamond. After drawing trumps, re-enter dummy with the queen of spades and ruff another diamond. Now, if the cards lie as you hope, the run of the black winners will inflict the squeeze.

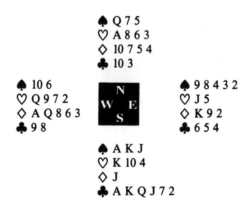

```
                    ♠ Q 7 5
                    ♡ A 8 6 3
                    ◇ 10 7 5 4
                    ♣ 10 3
    ♠ 10 6                         ♠ 9 8 4 3 2
    ♡ Q 9 7 2          N           ♡ J 5
    ◇ A Q 8 6 3     W     E        ◇ K 9 2
    ♣ 9 8              S           ♣ 6 5 4
                    ♠ A K J
                    ♡ K 10 4
                    ◇ J
                    ♣ A K Q J 7 2
```

There is no escape for West on the lie of the cards. But you had to make full use of dummy's entries, for the squeeze does not work until East's king of diamonds has been ruffed out.

Solution 5

The queen of hearts is an unwelcome sight, for you can be sure that East has the ace and ten to back it up. If you win with the king, West will be in a position to return a heart when he gains the lead and East will make at least three tricks in the suit.

A 3–3 club break would solve your problem but this must be unlikely. If you have to try for a ninth trick in spades West is bound to get in, for East would not have passed holding the king of spades along with his other goodies.

The only chance is a squeeze against West. You should play low from hand, allowing the heart queen to hold. If East continues with a low heart you can be confident that the suit is breaking 4–3. Win the trick, unblock the ace of diamonds and exit with the third heart.

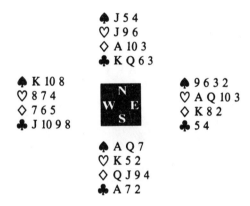

East cannot cash the thirteenth heart without setting up a squeeze against his partner. You discard spades from both hands, win the spade switch with the ace, and cash the winning diamond to give West the business.

If East refuses to cash the thirteenth heart, you have the tempo to set up your ninth trick in spades.

Solution 6

In spite of all your good cards there are only twelve tricks on view. The queen of diamonds could fall, of course, but if not you will have to rely on a squeeze. You might discard a club on the king of hearts and run all the trumps, discarding a heart and a diamond from dummy to achieve a criss-cross squeeze position.

But this would be a dubious method of play. Why rely on a squeeze that contains built-in ambiguity when there is a better option available. Here only East can have length in both minors, and a positional squeeze will grind East down with no ambiguity at all. Play low from dummy on the king of hearts, ruff in hand and run all the trumps, discarding a club or a diamond from the table. Now play off the ace and king of diamonds and the ace of hearts, and East will have to resign if he is in sole control of the minors.

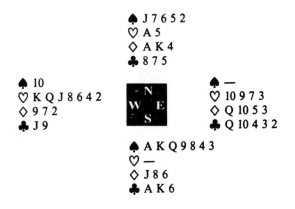

```
                    ♠ J 7 6 5 2
                    ♡ A 5
                    ◇ A K 4
                    ♣ 8 7 5
  ♠ 10                              ♠ —
  ♡ K Q J 8 6 4 2       N          ♡ 10 9 7 3
  ◇ 9 7 2          W         E     ◇ Q 10 5 3
  ♣ J 9                 S          ♣ Q 10 4 3 2
                    ♠ A K Q 9 8 4 3
                    ♡ —
                    ◇ J 8 6
                    ♣ A K 6
```

When you have a choice, opt for the squeeze that will not leave you guessing in the ending.

Solution 7

The jack of spades from East on the second round must be a suit-preference signal indicating something good in hearts—probably the king. But this does not mean that a heart switch must be the right defence. Think of the bidding for a moment. Declarer is likely to have six solid diamonds and the queen of hearts. He will have ten top tricks, in other words, and a heart switch will allow him to make his contract via a Vienna Coup and automatic squeeze against East. He will go up with the ace of hearts and run the diamonds, and partner will be unable to guard both hearts and clubs.

It is not a heart but a club switch that is required. If declarer has a singleton club, as seems almost certain on the bidding, this will break communications and destroy the squeeze.

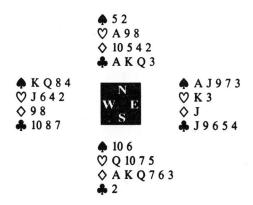

```
                  ♠ 5 2
                  ♡ A 9 8
                  ◇ 10 5 4 2
                  ♣ A K Q 3
    ♠ K Q 8 4                      ♠ A J 9 7 3
    ♡ J 6 4 2         N            ♡ K 3
    ◇ 9 8         W       E        ◇ J
    ♣ 10 8 7          S            ♣ J 9 6 5 4
                  ♠ 10 6
                  ♡ Q 10 7 5
                  ◇ A K Q 7 6 3
                  ♣ 2
```

This hand made an appearance during a practice match for Britain's 1983 European Championship team. In both rooms the defenders got it right, switching to a club at trick three to defeat the contract.

Solution 8

If the clubs fail to break you will be a trick short of your contract, but you can give yourself an extra chance if you are not in too great a hurry to test the clubs. Run the major suits first, discarding a club and a diamond from the table, and the inverted automatic squeeze will pinch either defender who happens to hold the queen of diamonds along with length in clubs.

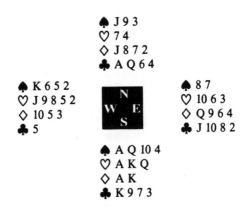

```
                    ♠ J 9 3
                    ♡ 7 4
                    ◇ J 8 7 2
                    ♣ A Q 6 4
  ♠ K 6 5 2                         ♠ 8 7
  ♡ J 9 8 5 2           N           ♡ 10 6 3
  ◇ 10 5 3          W       E       ◇ Q 9 6 4
  ♣ 5                   S           ♣ J 10 8 2
                    ♠ A Q 10 4
                    ♡ A K Q
                    ◇ A K
                    ♣ K 9 7 3
```

Do not fail to see that if you had played the king of clubs earlier 'to test the lie' the only squeeze left would have been a positional one, which would have failed on the actual lie of the cards.

Preserve those lovely split three-card menaces wherever possible.

Solution 9

Since East has shown up with eight cards in the majors West is likely to
have the minor-suit length. However, East would not have much of an
opening bid without the queen of diamonds, so it would be unwise to
rely on a straightforward finesse. West could have the ten of diamonds,
in which case it should be possible to transfer the task of guarding the
diamonds to him before squeezing him in the minors.

Alternatively, if East has only two diamonds a minor-suit squeeze
against West will succeed no matter who has the diamond queen. You
can check the position by ruffing a club. If East follows suit he can have
only two diamonds and you simply run the trumps to squeeze West.

If East discards on the third club, you must try to transfer the
diamond menace to West. The simplest method is to return to the ten
of spades and lead the jack of diamonds, winning with the ace when
East covers with the queen.

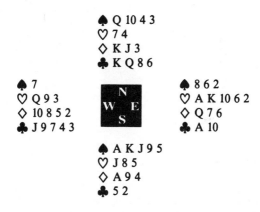

```
                    ♠ Q 10 4 3
                    ♡ 7 4
                    ◇ K J 3
                    ♣ K Q 8 6

    ♠ 7                           ♠ 8 6 2
    ♡ Q 9 3          N            ♡ A K 10 6 2
    ◇ 10 8 5 2    W     E         ◇ Q 7 6
    ♣ J 9 7 4 3      S            ♣ A 10

                    ♠ A K J 9 5
                    ♡ J 8 5
                    ◇ A 9 4
                    ♣ 5 2
```

Your split two-card menace in diamonds acts as the long menace, and
on the play of the last spade West is caught in a positional squeeze.

Solution 10

The only possible source of nourishment for the defence is in spades, and it seems natural to switch to a spade at this point. But the natural move is not always the right one. You can count declarer for five club tricks and three hearts. He is likely to have the ace of spades, a diamond finesse will bring his total up to eleven tricks, and partner is sure to be squeezed in spades and diamonds for the twelfth trick.

Partner's discard of the five of diamonds indicates an odd number of cards (clearly five) in the suit, so you can be confident that declarer has only one diamond. A diamond return into the jaws of dummy's tenace will give declarer nothing that is not his for the taking, and it will defeat the contract if partner has the king of spades.

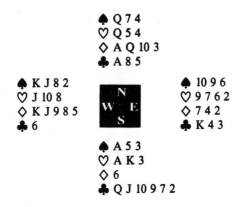

              ♠ Q 7 4
              ♡ Q 5 4
              ◇ A Q 10 3
              ♣ A 8 5

♠ K J 8 2   ♠ 10 9 6
♡ J 10 8   ♡ 9 7 6 2
◇ K J 9 8 5   ◇ 7 4 2
♣ 6   ♣ K 4 3

              ♠ A 5 3
              ♡ A K 3
              ◇ 6
              ♣ Q J 10 9 7 2

When you know that declarer has a singleton opposite a card of entry it is almost always right, for the purposes of squeeze defence, to attack that suit.

Solution 11

There will be no problem if the trumps are worth six tricks. If you have to lose a trump trick you will have to hope for a squeeze in spades and diamonds. From the opening lead it appears that East has the spade length, which rules out a positional squeeze. And a further spade lead will put paid to any idea of a normal automatic squeeze.

The only squeeze that is likely to work is a ruffing squeeze against East, and you must take care to preserve the required two entries in dummy. The correct move is to play the jack of hearts from dummy at trick two. If West produces the king he may knock out one of your entries with a spade or a diamond return, but you will still have the two you need.

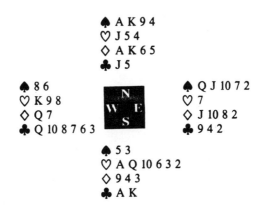

                ♠ A K 9 4
                ♡ J 5 4
                ◊ A K 6 5
                ♣ J 5

    ♠ 8 6   ♠ Q J 10 7 2
    ♡ K 9 8   N   ♡ 7
    ◊ Q 7   W   E   ◊ J 10 8 2
    ♣ Q 10 8 7 6 3   S   ♣ 9 4 2

                ♠ 5 3
                ♡ A Q 10 6 3 2
                ◊ 9 4 3
                ♣ A K

Suppose West returns a second spade when in with the king of hearts. You win with the king, run all the trumps but one, discarding diamonds from dummy, and cash the top clubs to inflict the ruffing squeeze.

If you play a small heart to your ten at trick two West may hold off smoothly. Now you will be tempted to squander one of dummy's entries to repeat the trump finesse. Winning with the king, West will knock out a third entry to kill your squeeze.

Solution 12

It seems likely that the heart finesse will work since East bid the suit, but there is no need to stake everything on this since East is marked with length in clubs as well.

The correct play is to duck this club lead to rectify the count for a possible squeeze. Win the next club, ruff a club high and run the trumps.

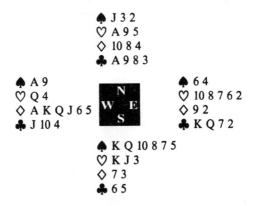

                    ♠ J 3 2
                    ♡ A 9 5
                    ◇ 10 8 4
                    ♣ A 9 8 3
    ♠ A 9   ♠ 6 4
    ♡ Q 4   ♡ 10 8 7 6 2
    ◇ A K Q J 6 5   ◇ 9 2
    ♣ J 10 4   ♣ K Q 7 2
                    ♠ K Q 10 8 7 5
                    ♡ K J 3
                    ◇ 7 3
                    ♣ 6 5

You discard the five of hearts on the last trump and East, in order to keep his club winner, has to reduce to two hearts. Now you play a heart to the ace and return the heart nine. When the queen does not appear you go up with the king, since you know that East's last card is the club king.

The 'count' squeeze provides a useful way of avoiding losing finesses.

Solution 13

It is inconceivable that South has leapt to six hearts with two losing spades in his hand. Corroboration is found in partner's play of the two of spades which indicates three cards in the suit. There is no point whatever in trying to cash another spade. Indeed this could be highly dangerous, helping declarer to isolate the spade stopper in your hand and set the scene for an eventual squeeze in spades and diamonds.

A diamond switch would be too risky, so the choice at trick two lies between a trump and a club. The trump is perhaps marginally safer since declarer is not likely to have a potential trump loser on this bidding.

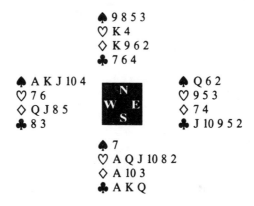

                 ♠ 9 8 5 3
                 ♡ K 4
                 ◊ K 9 6 2
                 ♣ 7 6 4

♠ A K J 10 4   ♠ Q 6 2
♡ 7 6   ♡ 9 5 3
◊ Q J 8 5   ◊ 7 4
♣ 8 3   ♣ J 10 9 5 2

                 ♠ 7
                 ♡ A Q J 10 8 2
                 ◊ A 10 3
                 ♣ A K Q

You see what happens if you play a second spade? Declarer ruffs, enters dummy with the king of hearts and ruffs a third spade. Left in sole charge of spades and diamonds, you are exposed to a squeeze on the run of the hearts.

After a heart or a club switch at trick two declarer lacks the entries to ruff two spades in hand. You can discard spades on the long hearts, leaving partner to look after the spade threat, and the squeeze fizzles out.

Solution 14

It is clear that East controls the fourth round of diamonds, and you can be confident that East also has the queen of hearts. With that card in addition to what he has already shown, West would surely have made himself heard in the bidding.

East must be squeezable; the only question concerns the type of squeeze that is required. If West had returned a heart you would have been able to organise a ruffing squeeze, using the ace of clubs and the queen of diamonds as the required entries to dummy. The club return put a stop to that plan, but you are left with an entry to dummy's heart suit in your hand and an entry to your diamond suit in dummy. This is the classical blocked position of the criss-cross squeeze. No further preparation is required. Just run the rest of the trumps, discarding a club and a heart from the table.

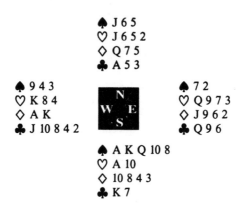

```
              ♠ J 6 5
              ♡ J 6 5 2
              ◊ Q 7 5
              ♣ A 5 3
♠ 9 4 3                        ♠ 7 2
♡ K 8 4          N            ♡ Q 9 7 3
◊ A K        W     E          ◊ J 9 6 2
♣ J 10 8 4 2     S            ♣ Q 9 6
              ♠ A K Q 10 8
              ♡ A 10
              ◊ 10 8 4 3
              ♣ K 7
```

No ambiguity arises in this instance because East is known to have started with four diamonds. If a diamond does not appear when you run the trumps, you cash the ace of hearts next.

Solution 15

You need the diamond finesse, but this still gives you only eleven tricks if the clubs do not break evenly. You might consider a minor-suit squeeze against West, who could well have club length along with his king of diamonds. Unfortunately the opening lead has taken out the only side entry to your hand.

This is the sort of situation where you have to arrange to win the last trump in your hand, enforcing the squeeze in the process. You need to ruff two hearts in dummy to achieve the partial dummy reversal. Finesse the ten of diamonds at trick two and then play a second heart, rectifying the count and preparing the ground for heart ruffs.

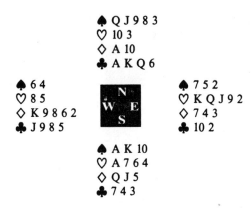

```
                    ♠ Q J 9 8 3
                    ♡ 10 3
                    ◇ A 10
                    ♣ A K Q 6
   ♠ 6 4                              ♠ 7 5 2
   ♡ 8 5             N                ♡ K Q J 9 2
   ◇ K 9 8 6 2    W     E             ◇ 7 4 3
   ♣ J 9 8 5         S                ♣ 10 2
                    ♠ A K 10
                    ♡ A 7 6 4
                    ◇ Q J 5
                    ♣ 7 4 3
```

You can win the trump return with the ten, ruff a heart, cash the ace of diamonds and play a trump to your king. When the trumps prove to be 3–2 you can safely ruff another heart. Now the play of a third spade to your ace draws the last trump and squeezes West at the same time.

When there are no squeeze entries in the side suits, always look to see if a trump will do instead.

Solution 16

Clearly you can cash four club tricks, but if you do you may find the contract to be unbeatable. Declarer must surely have the top spades and the king of diamonds for his bidding, which gives him eight top tricks. If you tighten up the timing by cashing your clubs you will inevitably be squeezed in the majors on the run of the diamonds.

The squeeze is not hard to foresee and an experienced defender will switch to the king of hearts at trick three. This upsets the timing of the squeeze and leaves declarer with too many losers.

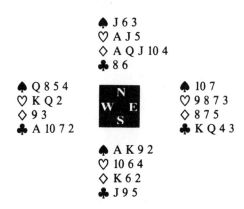

```
                    ♠ J 6 3
                    ♡ A J 5
                    ◇ A Q J 10 4
                    ♣ 8 6
♠ Q 8 5 4                          ♠ 10 7
♡ K Q 2            N               ♡ 9 8 7 3
◇ 9 3          W       E           ◇ 8 7 5
♣ A 10 7 2        S               ♣ K Q 4 3
                    ♠ A K 9 2
                    ♡ 10 6 4
                    ◇ K 6 2
                    ♣ J 9 5
```

When declarer takes the ace of hearts and runs the diamonds, you can discard one spade, one heart and the ace of clubs. Partner will keep his clubs, of course, and declarer will have no way of making more than eight tricks.

The initial lead of a heart honour and a later club switch defeats the contract just as easily, of course.

Solution 17

Having only ten tricks, you need to seek an eleventh in one of the major suits. Unfortunately West has left you with only one trump entry in dummy. East is marked with the king of spades on the bidding and it might be doubleton. You could cash the spade ace, enter dummy with the six of diamonds and return a small spade, hoping to bring down the king.

However, there are eight spades outstanding and only seven hearts, so if East has a doubleton it is rather more likely to be in hearts. If West has heart length (or both honours) along with the jack of spades, it will be possible to squeeze him in the majors.

Cash the spade ace, enter dummy with the diamond six and play the queen of spades, forcing a cover from East. After ruffing the king of spades, run the trumps and hope for the best.

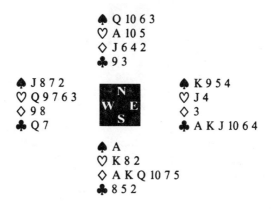

```
                  ♠ Q 10 6 3
                  ♡ A 10 5
                  ◇ J 6 4 2
                  ♣ 9 3
  ♠ J 8 7 2                        ♠ K 9 5 4
  ♡ Q 9 7 6 3      N              ♡ J 4
  ◇ 9 8         W     E           ◇ 3
  ♣ Q 7            S              ♣ A K J 10 6 4
                  ♠ A
                  ♡ K 8 2
                  ◇ A K Q 10 7 5
                  ♣ 8 5 2
```

On the play of the last diamond West is unable to hold the position in both majors and the game rolls home.

Solution 18

The defenders have found your weak spot and you have no more than eight top tricks. Clubs appear to be 5–3, which means that if you concede a diamond to either opponent you will lose too many tricks.

However, with West holding the club length it is quite probable that East has the stoppers in the red suit. This is a situation where the homicide squeeze may come to your aid. Cross to hand with the king of spades and play the jack of clubs, inviting West to run the suit.

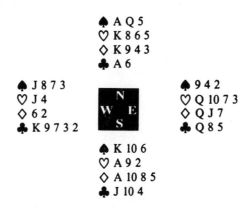

```
                    ♠ A Q 5
                    ♡ K 8 6 5
                    ◊ K 9 4 3
                    ♣ A 6
    ♠ J 8 7 3                        ♠ 9 4 2
    ♡ J 4            N               ♡ Q 10 7 3
    ◊ 6 2         W     E            ◊ Q J 7
    ♣ K 9 7 3 2      S               ♣ Q 8 5
                    ♠ K 10 6
                    ♡ A 9 2
                    ◊ A 10 8 5
                    ♣ J 10 4
```

If West cashes the clubs you can discard two hearts and a diamond from dummy and two diamonds from hand. The play of the spades will then mangle East's red-suit holdings.

It is no better for the defence if West chooses not to cash all of his clubs. You can win any switch and concede a diamond to East, setting up your ninth trick.

Solution 19

Declarer must have a long and solid diamond suit to account for his bidding. It would be a wild gamble to lead anything but partner's suit in this situation. A club lead may take out a vital entry and it is unlikely to do any harm.

It is normal to lead the top card from a doubleton, but against a grand slam you need not follow fashion slavishly. There is just a chance that the lowly four of clubs could be worth something in the end-game. The club two is the right choice.

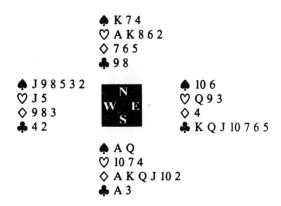

```
                    ♠ K 7 4
                    ♡ A K 8 6 2
                    ◇ 7 6 5
                    ♣ 9 8
  ♠ J 9 8 5 3 2                  ♠ 10 6
  ♡ J 5            N             ♡ Q 9 3
  ◇ 9 8 3      W       E         ◇ 4
  ♣ 4 2            S             ♣ K Q J 10 7 6 5
                    ♠ A Q
                    ♡ 10 7 4
                    ◇ A K Q J 10 2
                    ♣ A 3
```

The club lead takes out an entry, and South has to use the hearts as the long menace for his squeeze. He unblocks the spades, crosses to the ace of hearts, throws a heart on the spade king and runs the diamonds. But as soon as the nine of clubs is discarded from dummy East can throw his last club, keeping his heart guard. Your club four is big enough to contain the menace of declarer's three.

A non-club lead would have enabled South to choose clubs as the long menace. After a heart lead the sequence would be: heart ace, all the diamonds, discarding hearts, ace and queen of spades, heart to king, spade king to devastate partner.

So there was just one card to lead to beat the grand slam. Did you find it?

Solution 20

The 3–0 trump break is annoying. If you draw all the trumps you will have no more than eleven tricks including the king of spades. Yet you *must* draw trumps since you cannot safely ruff more than one club in hand with a low trump.

The only hope is an overtaking trump squeeze, and the play calls for careful timing. Cash the top diamonds and then play a spade towards your king.

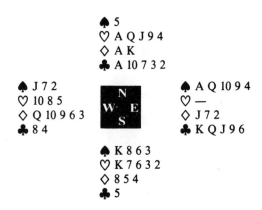

```
                    ♠ 5
                    ♡ A Q J 9 4
                    ◊ A K
                    ♣ A 10 7 3 2
   ♠ J 7 2                          ♠ A Q 10 9 4
   ♡ 10 8 5          N              ♡ —
   ◊ Q 10 9 6 3   W     E           ◊ J 7 2
   ♣ 8 4             S              ♣ K Q J 9 6
                    ♠ K 8 6 3
                    ♡ K 7 6 3 2
                    ◊ 8 5 4
                    ♣ 5
```

Suppose that East takes the ace of spades and returns a club (as good as anything). You ruff low, ruff a diamond in dummy, cash the queen of hearts and continue with the jack, drawing the last trump as you put the dilemma to East. If he reduces to a single club, you stay in dummy and ruff it out. If he comes down to two spades, you overtake with the king of hearts and establish an extra spade.

Note the need to cash the top diamonds before playing the spade. Otherwise, after a club return, you cannot balance the position by taking that diamond ruff.

A variation is possible if East plays low on the spade lead. Now you have to rectify the count by conceding a diamond.